Catherine J. Hall

The Leading Business Men of Middeltown, Portland, Durham and Middlefield

Catherine J. Hall

The Leading Business Men of Middeltown, Portland, Durham and Middlefield

ISBN/EAN: 9783337216139

Printed in Europe, USA, Canada, Australia, Japan

Cover: Foto ©Suzi / pixelio.de

More available books at **www.hansebooks.com**

MIDDLETOWN

AND ITS

LEADING

BUSINESS

MEN

THE

LEADING BUSINESS MEN

OF

MIDDLETOWN,

PORTLAND,

DURHAM AND MIDDLEFIELD.

ILLUSTRATED.

BOSTON:

MERCANTILE PUBLISHING COMPANY.

No. 98 Portland Street.

1890.

PREFACE.

In this historical and statistical review of the commercial and manufacturing interests of Middletown and vicinity, it has been our purpose in as thorough a manner as was possible to justly describe those enterprises which have contributed so largely during the last half century to the material advancement of the city. History plainly shows that many large cities owe their prosperity and growth chiefly to advantages of situation, great influx of foreign people, and similar causes; the present prosperity of this section, however, is due also to the genius and efforts of its people. A study of these facts, and of its varied mercantile interests, which are presented herewith, must show clearly, we think, the rich harvests that have been reaped from the exertions and foresight of the past, the present flourishing and influential position of Middletown and vicinity as a commercial centre, and its bright outlook for many lines of growth in the time to come.

MERCANTILE PUBLISHING COMPANY.

[See last page for Index.]

MIDDLETOWN AND ITS POINTS OF INTEREST

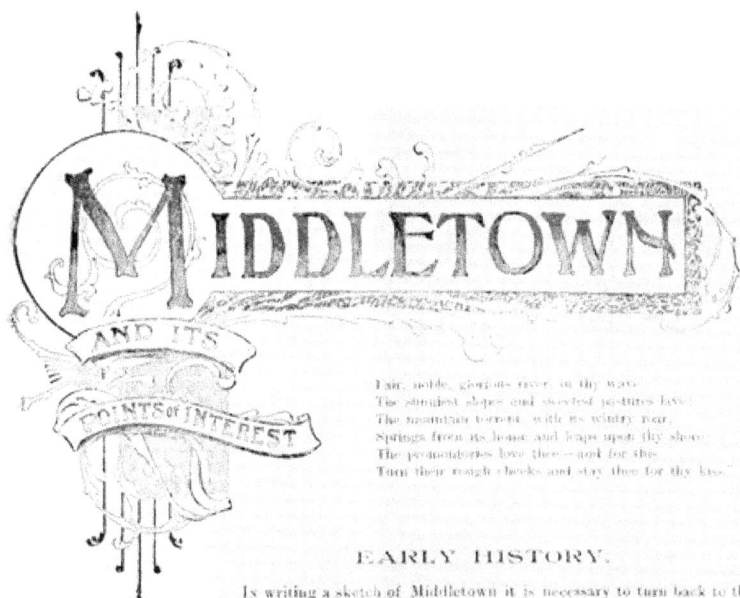

"Fair, noble, glorious river, in thy wave
The sunniest skies and shadiest pastures have;
The mountain torrent, with its wintry roar,
Springs from its home and leaps upon thy shore;
The promontories love thee—and for this
Turn their rough cheeks and stay thee for thy kiss."

EARLY HISTORY.

In writing a sketch of Middletown it is necessary to turn back to the time when the earliest English settlers came to the land now known as New England, and sought to make a home in what was then little more than a wilderness. It was in the year 1650 that the sons of the Pilgrims first came to this fair town of Mattabesett, or forest city, as it was called by the Indians, lying beside the broad Connecticut, noblest of New England rivers, nestling among the surrounding hills and almost hidden from view in the dense foliage of the forest trees. No pale-face had ever been seen in this region, and the Indian as yet was in full possession of his patrimony when the brave colonists made their appearance. After a few years the aspect of the place began to change —small clearings with rude huts or log houses might be seen, and the more substantial fortress or block-house, which served as a place of refuge in case of attack from their savage neighbors. For the most part, however, the two races lived peaceably side by side until with the advance of civilization, and in spite of his strength and bravery, the red man was obliged to retire before the white. English colonists from the vicinity of Boston had been invited in 1636 by the Indians who lived in the region about Hartford, to settle among them, with the expectation that the presence of the settlers might be a protection from their most dreaded enemies, the fierce Mohawks, and the equally warlike Pequots. Soon after this the Pequot war was undertaken and these hostile tribes almost destroyed. This was of the greatest importance to all the settlements on the Connecticut river, for it struck terror into the Indians throughout this region and prevented their rising against the English, to any extent, for nearly forty years.

During this time many settlements were made in Connecticut, but Mattabesett was for a time passed over, principally because it was the stronghold of a large tribe, whose powerful Sachem, Sawheag, was suspected of being an enemy to the English. This chief had his fortress on a hill situated about a mile back from the river, now known as Indian Hill, and dedicated as the place of final repose for the earthly remains of the descendants of these colonists.

It was not until 1650, after the subject had been under discussion for several years, that the settlement was actually made, all details concerning it being unobtainable, as the first pages of the town records are lost and others are nearly obliterated. It is known, however, that in 1651 the General Court "ordered sentenced and decreed that Mattabeseck shall bee a Towne, and that they shall make choyce of one of theire inhabitants, according to order in that case, that so bee may take the oath of a Constable, the next convenient season."

AIR LINE BRIDGE AND ISLAND.

"It is ordered that Mattabeseck and Norwaulk shall be rated this present year in their proporcon, according to the rule of rating in the Country, for their cattle and other visible estate, and that Norwaakk shall present to Mr. Ludlow and Mattabeseck to Mr. Wells in each Towne one inhabitant, to bee sworne by them Constables in their several Townes."

Two years later it was approved "that the name of the plantation commonly called Mattabeseck, should for time to come be called Middletown." This name was chosen, as some think, because the settlement lay between the towns up the river and Saybrook at its mouth; others that it was taken from some English town, whose name the colonists wished to perpetuate in their new home.

Before the commencement of the settlement Mr. Haynes, governor of Connecticut, had obtained from Sawheag a great part of the township, for a certain consideration, but it was not till many years after the death of this chieftain that the settlers came into full possession. The deed is as follows:

"This writing made the twenty-fourth of January, 1672, between Sepunnamoe, Joan, alias Weckpissick, Machize, Wesumpsha, Wamphauch, Spunno, Sachamas, Taccomhuit, proprietors of Middletown, alias Mattabesett, of the one part, and Mr. Samuel Wyllys, Capt. John Talcott, Mr. James Richards, and John Allyn, in behalf of the inhabitants of Middletown, on the other part, witnesseth, that the said Sepunnamoe, Joan, alias Weckpissick, Machize, Wesumpsha, Wamphauch,

Spunno, Sachamas, Taccomhuit, being
privy to and well acquainted with Sawheag, the great Sachem of Mattabesett,
his gift of great part of the township of
Middletown to the Honorable Mr. Hanyes
formerly, and for a further and full consideration to us now granted and paid, by
the said Mr. Samuel Wyllys, Capt. John
Talcott, Mr. James Richards and John
Allyn, have given, granted, bargained,
sold and confirmed, and by these presents
do fully and absolutely give, grant and
confirm unto the said gentlemen, all that
tract of land within these following abate-
ments, viz.: on Wethersfield bounds on
the north, on Haddam bounds on the
south, and to run from the great river
the whole breadth towards the east six
miles, and from the great river towards
the west so far as the General Court of
Connecticut hath granted, the bounds of
Middletown shall extend : to have and to
hold the aforementioned tract of land as
it is bounded, with all the meadows,
pastures, woods, underwood, stones, quarries, brooks, ponds, rivers, profits, commodities, and appurtenances whatsoever
belonging thereunto, unto the said Mr.
Samuel Wyllys, Capt. John Talcott, Mr.
James Richards and John Allyn, in behalf
and for the use of the inhabitants of the
town of Middletown, their heirs and
assigns forever ; always provided there
be three hundred acres of land within the
township of Middletown on the east side
of the Connecticut river, laid out, bounded,
and recorded to be and remain the heirs
of Sawheag and the Mattabesett Indians
and their heirs forever ; as also one parcel of land on the west side of Connecticut
river, formerly laid out to Sawseau, shall
be recorded and remain to the heirs of the
said Sawseau forever, anything in this
deed to the contrary notwithstanding.
And the foresaid Sepannamoe, Joan, alias
W e e k p i s s i c k, Machize, Wesumpsha,
Wamphauch, Spunno, Sachamas, Taccomhuit, for themselves, do covenant to and
with the said Mr. Wyllys, Capt. Talcott,
Mr. Richards and John Allyn, in behalf
of the inhabitants of Middletown, that
they the said Sepannamoe, Joan, Machize,

Bird's Eye View of Middletown, Connecticut.

Wesumpsha, etc., have only full power, good right and lawful authority to grant, bargain, sell and convey all and singular the before hereby granted, or mentioned to be granted premises, with their and every of their appurtenances, according as is above expressed, unto the said Mr. Wyllys, Capt. Talcott, Mr. Richards and John Allyn, in behalf of the inhabitants of Middletown aforesaid, their heirs and assigns forever, and that they, the said inhabitants of Middletown, shall and may by force and virtue of these presents, from time to time and at all times forever hereafter, lawfully, peaceably, and quietly, have, hold, use, occupy and possess and enjoy the aforesaid parcel of land with all its rights, members and appurtenances, and have, receive and take the rents, issues and profits thereof to their own proper use and behalf forever, without any let, suit, trouble or disturbance whatsoever of the said Sepunnamoe, Joan alias Weekpissick, Machize, Wesumpsha, Wampauch, Spuno, Sachamas, Taccombuit, their heirs or assigns, or of any other person or persons, claiming right by, from or under us, or any of us, or by the means, act consent, privity or procurement, and that free and clear, and freely and clearly acquitted, exonorated and discharged, or otherwise well and sufficiently saved and

MAIN STREET, LOOKING SOUTH FROM CORNER OF COURT STREET.

kept harmless by the said Sepunnamoe, Joan, Machize, Wesumpsha, Wampauch, Spuno, Sachamas, Taccombuit, their heirs, executors and administrators, of and from all former and other grants, gifts, bargains, sales, titles, troubles, demands, and incumbrances whatever, had, made, committed, suffered, or done by the said Sepunnamoe, Joan, Machize, Wesumpsha, Wamphauch, Spuno, Sachamas, Taccombuit. In witness hereof they have signed, sealed, and delivered this writing with their own hands the day and year first above written.

"Signed, sealed, and delivered in presence of us :

JOSEPH NASH,	SACHAMAS' MOTHER, × her mark,
GEORGE GRAVES,	SEPUNNAMOE, × his mark,
THOMAS EDWARDS,	JOAN alias WEEKPISSICK, × his mark,
ROBERT SANDFORD,	MAMACHIZE, his mark,
MESSEHEGEN, × his mark,	WESUMPSHA, his mark,
WANNOMOE, × his mark,	MAMPHAUEH, his mark,
TARRAMPGGGS, his mark.	SPUNNO, his mark,
PESSACESN, × his mark,	SACHAMAS, his mark."
TACCUMBUIT, his mark.	

The original is entered in the old Court Book of Records, folio 70, April 5th, 1673, "per me, John Allyn, Secretary."

"Middletown, April the eighth, one thousand six hundred and seventy-three, Pashuma, Rashiask, Massecumb, Robin, Pewamskin, with the consent of the natives, who signed and sealed the deed above written, were acknowledged to be interested in this land reserved to them therein and for themselves, their heirs and assigns, did and by these presents do give, grant, and confirm unto the inhabitants of Middletown, their heirs, and assigns, forever, all their right, title, interest, in all that tract of land

granted by the above written deed unto the said inhabitants of M i d d l e t o w n fully and largely as is expressed in the above written deed, as witness our hands the day and year first above written.

"Signed, sealed, and delivered in the presence of us :

NATHANIEL WHITE,
JOHN HALL,
SAMUEL STOCKING,
RASHIASK'S × MARK,
PASHUMA'S × MARK,
MASSECUMB'S × MARK,
ROBIN'S × MARK,
PEWAMSKIN'S × MARK."

CORNER WASHINGTON AND HIGH STREETS.

"The above written is a true record of the deed of the land within the township of Middletown from the Indian proprietors.   Per me, JOHN HALL, Recorder."

As the colonists made advances in clearing and cultivation, the Indians gradually moved farther away, though they held lands in the neighborhood until 1713, and made the Sabethe or Little river the head of navigation for their canoes, as they made trips up and down the Connecticut in search of food. It is not absolutely known who were the first settlers, the earliest entry now extant being a vote for building a meeting-house, dated February 2, 1652. Hitherto their place of worship had been under the shade of a grand old elm, which stood at the entrance of the grave-yard. The meeting-house was soon built, and though a rude building, only twenty feet square, it served its purpose for nearly thirty years, when a new one was built. The settlement, which originally included the present towns of Chatham, Portland, Cromwell, Middlefield and a small part of Berlin, was sixteen miles in length, from east to west, and nine in breadth from north to south, and was made under the constitution of 1639, which allowed the colonists to elect their own officers and unite with others for the election of officers for the commonwealth. This was superseded by the charter of Charles II., procured by Governor Winthrop from that monarch, which gave the people the legal management of all their own concerns. They elected their officers wisely, choosing men of high moral standing, who in many instances, continued in these positions till their death. A few of these prominent men, who were highly honored by their fellow-citizens, may be here mentioned. Nathaniel White, who was one of the first magistrates ; Giles Hamlin, his son John, and his grandson, Jabez ; Seth Wetmore, Samuel W. Dana, Asher Miller, John Hall, Robert Webster, Nathaniel Brown, George Hubbard, etc.

In 1670 there were but fifty-two houses in the town and thirty-five surnames, many of which are now borne by prominent citizens. After this time the population increased, and by 1750 six parishes were formed in the township. These were all Congregational societies, and it was not for some time afterwards that other denominations settled in Middletown. The people were assembled for worship by the beat of a drum, given to the town by Mr. Giles Hamlin, and the meeting-house was guarded during service by a small force of armed men, as a security from attack of the Indians. The colonists were of a practical turn of mind and had a fair amount of learning. As early as 1676, when their means were small, they felt the necessity for having a school wherein to educate the children, and an agreement was made to pay £25 to a Mr. Webb for teaching school one year.

In October, 1646, the court granted permission to build a bridge over "ferrye river," now Little river, and in 1688, Francis Whittemore and his heirs were permitted to receive "the fare of two pence money for each time for horse and man and load, and one pennie a time a single person."

One of the early ordinances adopted was "A Bye-Law Restraining Swine and Geese from Going at large in the City."

The whipping-post, which stood at the South Green, was used as late as 1825 for the punishment of minor offences, and afterwards as a sign-post, for posting notices.

During the first century, the financial condition of the people did not greatly improve. They almost all looked to their clearings and forests for means of support, but gradually various industries sprang up, such as ship-building, mining and quarrying. In 1680, there was but one merchant in the place—a single vessel of seventy tons was owned in Middletown, and only one other, of ninety tons was owned on the river, that being at Hartford. It was not until the latter part of the eighteenth century, or during the fifty years preceding the Revolution, that any amount of wealth was amassed in the community. A profitable trade was opened with the West Indies, during which time many Middletown merchants laid the foundations of large fortunes, foremost among whom were Richard Alsop, Col. Matthew Talcott, George Phillips, Elijah and Nehemiah Hubbard, Genl. Comfort Sage, and numerous others. This trade stimulated agriculture as well as domestic manufactures, and the increase in the population was very apparent. Ship-building now became an important occupation, grist-mills, saw-mills, fulling-mills for dressing home-made cloth, were erected, and the different trades, such as carpenters, blacksmiths, wheelwrights, shoemakers, etc., multiplied. The best lands were cultivated and yielded abundant crops of corn and other grains. Quantities of provisions and great numbers of cattle and horses were sent to the West Indies, and in return, the merchants received sugar, molasses, rum, and various articles of valuable merchandise from these ports.

The West India trade, and almost all other trade was suspended during the Revolutionary War, when all able-bodied men were called upon to deliver their country from the yoke of the oppressor. Few towns suffered more from the calamities of this war than Middletown, owing to the almost total interruption of its foreign commerce. The people, however, did not for this or any other reason hesitate in the discharge of what they considered their duty to their country. They obeyed the summons cheerfully, and during this long and bloody war, many a gallant Middletown man gladly lay down his life in defence of the rights of the land. All trade was willingly broken off with England, though this meant poverty for many families. Every energy was bent upon sending men and supplies to our army. When, with the battle of Lexington in April, 1775, the war began in earnest, a company of light infantry, constituted at Middletown the previous year, with Capt. Meigs in command, marched immediately to the environs of Boston "completely uniformed and equipped," where Capt. Sage, another Middletown man, was already in charge of a company of light horse.

At this time a lead mine in this town, was in the hands of the British. It was found that Colonel James, one of their officers, had prepared a quantity of the ore for exportation, which the government of Connecticut now seized for its own use.

At this same time the brilliant scheme for taking Ticonderoga was formed in Connecticut, many Middletown men taking part in it and furnishing funds for the purpose, foremost among whom were Samuel Holden Parsons, Sam'l Wyllys and Silas Deane.

In the memorable battle of Bunker Hill, which occurred the following June, and in the other battles of this war, Middletown furnished her quota of brave soldiers, a large number serving in Washington's army. It is recorded that "they signalized themselves in all the achievements and were distinguished for their sufferings as well as for their valor."

During the year 1776, the standing militia of Connecticut were subjected to five heavy drafts, and it would be easier to say who did not go to the war, than to enumerate those who went from this town. Their privations and hardships were very great. Many were taken prisoners and died without seeing their homes again. It would be difficult to tell all that the people of this neighborhood did during this long struggle. They showed brave and stout hearts and proved their devotion to their country to the utmost. Of those who died in prison the names are known of James Smith, Abijah Kirby, Nathan Edwards and Reuben Kirby. These are only a few of the great number whose names are not recorded. It is impossible to ascertain how many officers and men from this town were in the Continental army, for many of the records of this time have been lost, and but few names remain. Among the most prominent figures during this period was Captain Return Jonathan Meigs. He was made captain in 1774, major the following year, and he accompanied Arnold on the expedition against

SOLDIERS' MONUMENT, IN INDIAN HILL CEMETERY.

the city of Quebec. Colonel Meigs returned to Middletown after the war, where he remained till 1787, when he moved to Marietta, Ohio. At the time of his death, in 1823, he was Indian agent among the Cherokees, who named him "The White Path."

With the renewal of hostilities on the northern border in 1812, Middletown again took a prominent part. The hero of the memorable battle fought at Lake Champlain, and the commandant of the United States naval forces there, was the gallant Captain McDonough, of this town. We would refer our readers for a detailed account of this brilliant victory, to the admirable description given by J. Fenimore Cooper. Our forces were greatly inferior to the British, but Capt. McDonough so encouraged his men, that they fought with the courage of despair. The victory was great and triumphant. The stand taken by Capt. McDonough was the subject of universal admiration. He was promoted for his services, and received numerous gifts from different States and towns, besides the usual medal from Congress.

Commodore McDonough was in the navy until just before his death, when, from ill health, he was forced to resign his command of the *Constitution*. He left Gibraltar, and sailed for home in October, 1825, and on the 10th of November died at sea. His loss was deeply mourned by the country at large, and his remains were accompanied with military pomp to their last resting-place. Some of his descendents are at this day among the best-known citizens of Middletown.

GROWTH OF THE CITY AND ITS INDUSTRIES DURING THIS CENTURY.

The Revolution having come to a successful issue, commerce once more began to revive.

A petition dated January 15, 1784, was signed and presented to the legislature the following May, asking that Middletown should be invested with city privileges. The signers alleged that "many inconveniences were felt by them, as well as by strangers, for want of a due regulation of the police of the town," and that many other regulations for the commercial interests of the place were impossible to accomplish without a separate and special jurisdiction. This petition was granted, and Middletown, together with Hartford, New Haven, New London and Norwich, were constituted cities in May, 1784. Jabez Hamlin was elected mayor at the first city meeting that same year, and con-

HIGH STREET, LOOKING NORTH.

tinued to hold the office until his death, in 1791. Besides the commercial revival, the city itself began to grow. In 1815, there were in the city 299 dwellings and 353 families,—in 1850, there were 603 dwelling-houses and 718 families.

As a place of residence and natural beauty, Middletown has few equals and has always been justly celebrated. Washed along its eastern border by the majestic and beautiful Connecticut River, on the north by the winding Sabethe or Little River, bounded on the west by a chain of picturesque hills, abounding in streams and rivulets in every direction—easily accessible by land and water, endowed with a fertile soil and healthful climate, what place could be more attractive to settle in and enjoy a peaceful life? But no place thrives by remaining stationary, and soon churches, banks, a court-house, custom-house, jail, etc., were built, besides a number of factories.

In consequence of the failure of foreign commerce, which gradually died out after the Revolution, numerous enterprising men were obliged either to move away, or resort to manufacturing. Many chose this latter alternative, and the result is, that Middletown, from having been the centre of the great West India trade, now became the manufacturing centre of the State.

One branch of foreign commerce was still carried on with great success for many years. This was the trade with China, conducted by the house of Russell & Co., founded by Mr. Samuel Russell in 1824. This house still exists and is said to have the best credit of any house engaged in the business. Some of the factories were in operation before the close of the war, especially those for making powder and fire-arms. In 1810, Col. North started a pistol manufactory at Staddle Hill, a suburb of Middletown, which was the first manufactory of government pistols in this country. For many years the product was about 10,000 pistols yearly. During the war of 1812, every available spot in the vicinity was selected for the erection of factories to supply government demands, and here was the chief and almost only source of government supplies. Swords, rifles, muskets, revolving fire-arms, pistols, powder, etc., were all made here, and several hundred thousand dollars of government money found its way annually into the old Middletown Bank and the United States Branch Bank. Multitudes of other manufacturing interests have sprung up during the present century. Prominent among them, and by far the largest is the Russell Manufacturing Co., which makes heavy cotton belting and hose, cotton and worsted webbing and suspenders, satin and silk ribbons, etc., etc. The large establishment of Messrs. W. & B. Douglas, where are made patent metallic pumps and hydraulic rams, which have gained the reputation of being the best pump and water elevator now in use, and are shipped largely to all parts of this country and Europe. The Stiles & Parker Press Co., the Middletown Plate Co., the Palmer Co. for manufacturing netting, Wm. Wilcox & Co. who make superior plate locks, and many others too numerous to mention in this sketch, some of which are noticed more at length in another part of this publication. They include factories making rubber goods, blind fasteners, sashes and blinds, silk, hardware, saddlery, harness trimmings, machinery,

Union Green and Soldiers' Monument.

tools of various kinds, soap, articles of ivory and bone, etc., etc. All these industries represent many thousands of dollars annually, and in addition to these, the retail trade has made great progress of late years. There are well-stocked and furnished stores, where nearly every article needed for consumption, apparel and household use may be obtained.

In addition to these sources of industry, there is a good deal of mineral wealth in and about Middletown. It consists of lead, sulphur, a small amount of copper and silver, and a number of other minerals, besides feldspar quarries, which have been worked from time to time.

Again with regret we have to record how the peacefulness and prosperity of this city was disturbed, by the sound of war being heard throughout the land. Every American citizen knows the sad story of our Civil War, the hardships endured without a murmur, and the great courage shown on both sides, the many bloody battles fought and the brave men killed on the field, or worse still, left to die a lingering death in the wretched prisons. The call to arms was instantly answered by men throughout New England, ready and eager to fight for their beloved flag.

The news of the bombardment of Fort Sumter created intense excitement in Middletown. Mass meetings were held, and the local companies, the Mansfield Guards and an artillery company began to prepare for active service, and to enroll recruits. A full company of volunteers, known as the Mansfield Guards, marched from Middletown, April 24, 1861, under the command of Captain David Dickerson, going first to New Haven, and then to Washington. Two other companies, the Wesleyan Guards and the Union Guards, were formed, and left for the seat of war on the 16th of May. A committee, made up of some of the most influential men of the town, was formed for the purpose of equipping and uniforming the soldiers. The ladies also were untiring in their endeavors. They organized an aid society for supplying the soldiers with such articles of comfort as the government could not furnish, thereby relieving the suffering and gladdening the heart of many a weary soldier. Middletown sent many of her foremost citizens to swell the army, numbers of whom won renown for their gallant conduct. Others there were who never returned, and who are still mourned by their fellow-townsmen as well as by their immediate families. Though our space is necessarily limited, no sketch of Middletown, however brief, would be complete without special mention of one of her citizens, who was a notable hero in the late war, and nobly gave his life in defense of his country. This was General Joseph K. F. Mansfield. He was a prominent figure in many battles, both in the Mexican and the Civil War. In the former he was intrusted with the responsible post of chief engineer of the army commanded by Major General Taylor, during the years 1846-7. He was particularly distinguished in the defense of Fort Brown, receiving the brevet of major, and at Monterey, September 21, 22 and 23, 1846, he was severely wounded, and was brevetted lieutenant-colonel for gallant conduct. Five months later, at Buena Vista, he received the brevet of colonel. At the outbreak of the Civil War, he was chosen inspector general of the army, with the rank of colonel. In April, 1861, he was placed in command of the department of Washington, and at once commenced the work of fortifying the capital, receiving the appointment of brigadier-general of volunteers the following month. All the forts around Washington were engineered by General Mansfield, and built under his supervision. He was in command of the battle of Newport News, led our forces in the capture of Norfolk, May 10, 1862, and was soon after promoted to the rank of major-general. He was assigned to the command of a division in the army of the Potomac, September 10th, at the head of which a week later, while encouraging his troops at the battle of Antietam, he received wounds from which he died the next day, September 18, 1862. His remains were brought home, and amid the mourning of the entire population, he was buried with full military honors in the beautiful cemetery on Indian Hill, of which the city may be justly proud. A fine monument has been erected to his memory, and every year, on Decoration Day, his grave, together with those of all the gallant dead who perished in the war, are decked with flags and flowers in memory of that sad time. A fine soldier's monument, costing $11,000 (of which the cut on page nine gives some idea), has since been erected to commemorate the deeds of these brave men. Situated in a picturesque spot, on a mound in the midst of the Union Green, the bronze figure of an ideal volunteer infantry soldier, in the regulation uniform and overcoat, overlooks the passer-by. The figure is raised upon a pedestal of Quincy granite, the whole being nineteen feet eight inches in height. Tablets of bronze on the sides of the pedestal, bear the names of the 110 Middletown men who were killed in action, or died from wounds, and the following inscriptions :

"Their Heroic Valor Insures Our Lasting Peace"
"Honor to the Brave."
"We Cherish Their Memory."
"Erected by the town of Middletown in memory of her fallen Sons, 1874."

About the base four twelve pound bronze cannons, taken from the Confederate army, and sixteen cannon balls are placed.

The statue was dedicated June 24, 1874, with suitable ceremonies.

When peace reigned once more, people tried to pick up the broken threads of their lives, for a long time, with but indifferent success. But gradually the tide of prosperity set in once more, and Middletown is to-day a well-to-do place of 15,110 inhabitants, showing an increase of 3,408 during the last ten years.

MIDDLETOWN OF TO-DAY.

Middletown enjoys unusual facilities for transportation both by land and water. The harbor is fine, and the river deeper here than it is beyond, so that vessels drawing ten feet of water can ascend to this city with perfect ease. It is the third city in the State for freight exports, ranking in this respect, before Hartford. A great deal of freight is taken to New York by steamboat, which leaves daily, with freight and passengers. The railroad connections are the Connecticut Valley, the Air Line Division of the New York, New Haven and Hartford railroad, and the Middletown branch of the Hartford and New Haven railroad. Trains arrive at and depart from the new railroad station, built a few years ago on the site of the old Mortimer House, perhaps better known by the name of its late owner, Captain William G. Hackstaff. Mr. Philip Mortimer built this house near the river, ornamented and planted the several acres of ground, surrounding it with shade trees, and opened it to the public. It was an object of admiration to everyone, and it is an interesting fact, that when a portion of the

MAIN STREET LOOKING SOUTH FROM WASHINGTON STREET.

French army in the Revolution, were on their way from the East to Washington's encampment, they stopped over Sunday in Middletown, and the officers amused themselves by dancing under these trees, and cutting the names of Washington, Lafayette and other interesting characters in the bark.

Now the place is completely metamorphosed. The trees have been felled, and a brick building stands in the place of the former wooden one. A fine drawbridge spans the river at this point, built and used exclusively by the Air Line railroad.

Other buildings are the court house, built in 1832, the second building of the kind in Middletown since the county of Middlesex was formed, which contains the records of the city and town, and the offices of the town clerk and selectmen; the post-office, established in 1775, the custom-house, built in 1834, the first floor now being used for the post-office; the county jail, a stone building containing twelve cells, built in 1848, and the alms-house, which was first occupied in 1814.

BANKS

The banking interests of Middletown are extensive and rank high in the State. The first one, the Middletown National Bank, dates from 1795, Elijah Hubbard having been the first president; the Middlesex County National Bank, organized in 1830, by special charter from the legislature; the Central National Bank, dating from 1851, and the First National Bank, from 1864. There are two savings banks, the Middletown Savings Bank, founded in 1825, and the Farmers and Mechanics Savings Bank, incorporated in 1858, and two banking companies, the Middlesex Banking Company, incorporated by special act of legislature in 1872, which deals largely in Western real estate and loans, with a capital of $600,000, and the C. E. Jackson Company.

A bank protective association was organized in 1880, for the protection of the banks against burglars. An electric burglar alarm connects all the banks with headquarters, and assistants are in constant attendance, who are sent out in case of alarm.

Insurance interests are in no way neglected in Middletown. There are five companies, The Insurance Co., The Fire Insurance Co., The Marine Fire Insurance Co., and the Middlesex Fire Assurance Co., the first having been founded at the beginning of the century.

THE PRESS

Several daily papers have been issued at different times in this city, which were eventually discontinued. At the present time two papers are published daily. They are the *Daily Herald*, issued since 1883 by the Middletown Publishing Co., and the *Penny Press*.

The weeklies are of longer standing. The *Sentinel* and *Witness*, formed by the union in 1832, of the *American Sentinel* and the *Witness*, has always been the organ of the Democratic party in Middlesex county. It is issued every Saturday from its office near the corner of Main and Centre streets. A second weekly paper, called the *Constitution*, was first issued in January, 1838, by Abner Newton. It was purchased in 1877 by Charles W. Church, son-in-law of the original owner, and is still conducted by him.

THE WATER SUPPLY

The city water works are located on the Laurel Brook, on the division line between Middletown and Middlefield. They were constructed in 1866, under the supervision of George H. Bishop, a native of Middletown and a skillful civil engineer, who was at that time president of the board of water commissioners. The entire property covers an area of eighty-six acres, seventy-two of these being used as a reservoir, which has a capacity for 200,000,000 gallons. It was constructed at a cost of $229,436.82. The fall of water to Main street is 168 feet. The water is used freely by the citizens for all purposes, it having been analyzed by an eminent chemist, Prof. Atwater of the Wesleyan University, who pronounced it "as pure and wholesome as we need wish."

THE FIRE DEPARTMENT

The people of Middletown have always taken great precautions against fire, and the records show that there are few cities in the United States, of the same population, where so few fires have occurred. The first fire company was organized in 1803. The annals say, that each resident owner of a house, store or office was obliged to "keep in constant readiness and repair one good leather bucket containing not less than two gallons," and any person setting up a stove in a house, without the examination and approbation of the fire wardens, was to pay a fine of $2. Some sections of the ordinances dated 1803, relating to "the Preservation of said City from Fire," are very curious,—notably, Section 23:

"That if any person whatever shall be found smoking of segars in any highway in the city, he shall forfeit and pay the sum of one dollar." Section 9 reads, "It is also enjoined of the Inhabitants on the Cry of Fire in the Night, forthwith to place a lighted candle at one or more of the Front Windows of their respective Houses."

The present fire department consists of one hook and ladder company, and three hose companies, The O. V. Coffin Hook and Ladder Co., The Douglas Hose Co., The Hubbard Hose Co., and the Forest City Hose Co. They have all rendered most valuable services to the city, and the whole department is under the charge of Chief Engineer F. W. Willey

EDUCATIONAL FACILITIES.

Educational matters have been looked upon since the earliest times, as being of the utmost importance in Middletown. Numerous private schools were opened, followed by Captain Partridge's Military and Scientific Academy, an excellent school, which gained a widespread reputation. There are now numbers of district schools, besides a fine, large high school, built of brick and stone, situated

WESLEYAN UNIVERSITY. (THE DORMITORY).

on College street, where the course of study is very thorough and complete, and the staff of teachers exceedingly fine. The benefits of the high school have been very great, by bringing the higher English branches, and the elementary branches of Latin and Greek within the means of all. The tuition fees at first very moderate, are now entirely done away with.

"Born as it were in the Lyceum of Capt. Partridge's Academy," is the WESLEYAN UNIVERSITY, one of the largest educational institutions in the State. It was founded in 1831, under the direction of the Methodist Church, the first president, Rev. Willbur Fisk, D.D., and the officers all being members of this body. The buildings are large, numerous and handsome, built chiefly of brown stone from the Portland quarries. These comprise a handsome memorial chapel, dedicated to thirteen of the alumni and students, who among the 153 from the university, had been in service in the Federal armies and fallen; the Orange Judd Hall of Natural Science; the library erected by Isaac Rich, with a capacity for 100,000 volumes; dormitories, and an observatory which is fitted with one of Alvan Clark's finest refracting telescopes. Their location, on High street, at the head of College street, is exceedingly beautiful. A fine campus stretches in front of the buildings, shaded by enormous elms, the whole effect being most picturesque. This institution is very wealthy, and is continually receiving large bequests from people belonging to the Methodist society. The college property, including buildings, appurtenances, fixtures and endowment funds, amounts to $1,308,186. There are twenty-three members of the faculty, and the body of students in 1889, numbered 231, more than ever before. The college has graduated 1500 men, 1200 of whom are still living. Many of them are occupying the most influential positions in Church, State and school. The library now numbers 38,500 volumes. Property directly opposite the campus on High street has been recently purchased and fitted up as a dormitory for the young lady students, and it is proposed to build a new gymnasium. Five houses have been purchased or built, and handsomely fitted up by the different fraternities connected with the university, to serve as club houses. These are mostly situated near the college buildings, and form quite a feature of that part of the town.

The president is the Rev. Bradford Paul Raymond, D.D., Ph.D., elected in 1888. He is a man exceptionally well fitted to fill the position, and the college promises to increase in prosperity and popularity under his management.

WESLEYAN UNIVERSITY, MIDDLETOWN.

ORANGE JUDD HALL.   LIBRARY.   CHAPEL.   OBSERVATORY.

Another institution is the BERKELEY DIVINITY SCHOOL, designed for the training of young men for the ministry of the Protestant Episcopal Church. It was first established in Hartford, in connection with Trinity College, the Right Rev. John Williams, D.D., bishop of Connecticut, and now presiding bishop of the church, having held the position of chancelor and dean from the beginning. After the death of the Rev. S. F. Jarvis, his house, a three-story brick building, situated at the corner of Main and Washington streets, which is very large and had been built for a hotel in 1812, was offered to the Berkeley School as a gift, on condition that it should be removed permanently to Middletown. This offer was accepted, and the bishop has since made it his residence, part of the building being used for libraries, class-rooms and sleeping rooms for the students. It may be interesting to note the fact that when General Lafayette was passing through this portion of the country in 1825, a large public reception was given in his honor, in this house, then the Washington Hotel. An exceedingly beautiful chapel near by, called St. Luke's Chapel, was built in 1861 and presented to the Berkeley School in memory of Dr. Mütter, by his widow, who was a native of Middletown, and a lady well known for her generosity. Other buildings connected with the school are a two-story building, used as a dormitory for students, a gymnasium, and the "Wright House," just beyond the chapel, so called from the original owner, Joseph Wright. It was built between the years 1745 and 1750, of brick made at Newfield. This is the first instance of American brick being used for building, all such material having been imported from England before that date. The library of the Berkeley School numbers over 17,000 volumes, many of them being of great value, and the institution has an endowment fund of $173,216.00.

THE RUSSELL LIBRARY.

The educational facilities of Middletown are also enhanced by the Free Russell Library, the generous gift to the city, in 1875, of the late Mrs. Samuel Russell, in memory of her husband. This building is of Portland stone, situated at the corner of Broad and College streets on the old site of the Episcopal Church, and is in fact, remodelled from it. It comprises a large number of valuable books

BROAD STREET, OPPOSITE RUSSELL LIBRARY.

of reference, a circulating library, and a recently enlarged hall, in which entertainments are given. The book cases have a capacity for 25,000 volumes. Mrs. Russell expended $20,000 in remodelling this building, $6,000 in books, and endowed it with $40,000. The income goes to defray the expenses and to purchase new books.

Another gift of Mrs. Russell, is the pretty brown stone mortuary chapel, situated near the entrance of Indian Hill Cemetery.

CONNECTICUT HOSPITAL FOR THE INSANE.

By far the most extensive institution in this city, or in the State, is the Connecticut Hospital for the Insane, which was opened April 30, 1868. Situated on high ground, at some little distance from the city, it commands a magnificent view of the river in either direction. The buildings are numerous, handsome and of enormous size, the original ones being built of Portland stone, the later ones of brick. They comprise three distinct buildings, known as the main, middle and south hospitals, besides an annex and five cottages. A steam-engine of twenty-five-horse power is connected with them, and is used for supplying artificial ventilation and other purposes. A beautiful lawn, edged with fine trees and dotted here and there with fountains and beds of bright-hued flowers, slopes down to the road, and is an object of admiration to every passer-by. The total of appropriations at the close of 1883 was $788,943. In June, 1888, the receipts amounted to $316,939.38. The average number of patients present during the year 1887-8 amounted to 1292, an increase of 800 upon ten years ago. The resident officers are aided in the care of the patients by 179 assistants. All patients who are able, are employed in some way, averaging about half of the men and forty per cent. of the

CONNECTICUT HOSPITAL FOR THE INSANE, MIDDLETOWN.

women. Numerous entertainments are provided for the patients—music, lectures, etc., etc., and a number of newspapers and periodicals. The success of this institution has been very great since its formation, and the present superintendent, James Olmstead, M.D., is eminently fitted for carrying on this vast work.

CONNECTICUT INDUSTRIAL SCHOOL FOR GIRLS.

This is not a State Institution, but a private charity, incorporated and employed by the State for the custody, guardianship and instruction of viciously inclined girls, between the ages of eight and sixteen years, or those who are considered in danger of falling into habits of vice. Each one committed by legal process the State treats as wards, and pays for at the rate of $2.75 a week. Its design is not that of a prison, but a temporary place of custody and instruction, where the children can receive a good moral, mental and physical training, which they could not have elsewhere and which will enable them later to fill good positions, and become useful members of society. Each girl is kept in the institution until she is twenty-one years of age, unless sooner discharged according to law. The school was incorporated in 1868, and received its first inmates in January, 1878. Its present condition is most prosperous and encouraging. It has a beautifully located, well cultivated and stocked farm, five large houses or homes accommodating two hundred inmates, a school building, chapel, box factory, superintendent's and farmer's house, barns and other buildings. There are thirteen buildings in all, eight of brick and five of wood. Seven hundred and eighty-nine pupils were received from January 1, 1870 to June, 1887, and the number during this latter year amounted to 212. The superintendent is Mr. W. G. Fairbanks. He receives valuable aid in the management of the institution from his wife, and a competent force of matrons and teachers.

Among the charities on a smaller scale, are the St. Luke's Home for destitute and aged women, and the Middlesex County Orphan's Home, both most excellent institutions.

RELIGIOUS BODIES.

As was generally the case in New England colonies, the Congregationalists were the first religious body to settle in Middletown. As already mentioned, they soon built a rude meeting-house. The society was formed November 4, 1668, eighteen years after the first settlement of the town, with Nathaniel Collins as pastor. It was the seventeenth planted in the colony of Connecticut, and is nearly one hundred years older than any other in the town. The society is known as the "First Church of Christ in Middletown." The present church is the fifth that has been built. It is an imposing structure on Court street near Main, and was built in 1872.

Next in date comes the Protestant Episcopal Church, or the American branch of the Church of England. There was no regular parish until 1750, and the first church was built two years later. The second stood on the site of the Russell Library, and the present handsome edifice is situated on Main street.

A second Congregational society formed itself in 1751, the members calling themselves "Strict Congregationalists." The present church edifice was dedicated in 1830. It is situated at the corner of Main street and the South Green.

On the south side of the green, is the Methodist Episcopal Church. This form of worship was held by circuit preachers for some time before the erection of their first church in 1805. The congregation has increased very rapidly since the establishment of the Wesleyan University, as the faculty, their families, and most of the students are connected with it. The present building is of brick, and was erected in 1828.

The Baptist society was formed in this city in 1795. They built their first house of worship in 1809. The present one was built in 1842 at a cost of $12,500.

The Universalists first held service in the Lancasterian School House, for about ten years, when in 1839, a house of worship was built at the corner of Main and College streets.

A short distance west of the University stands the African Methodist Episcopal Church. The society was organized in 1826, and the following year a church was built entirely by subscription.

An imposing edifice is the Roman Catholic Church. In 1843 they erected a brick building for the purpose, fronting the north green. It was soon found insufficient to accommodate the members, and accordingly a larger one of Gothic architecture, and of Portland stone, was begun on the same site, in 1850.

In 1884 the second centenary of the city was celebrated. A large concourse of people was present, the population of the town being increased, for the time, to double its size. Addresses were made, odes read, and songs sung. All the civic organizations of the city were represented in full force, streets and buildings were gay with bunting, and the procession was a remarkably fine one. Those who had heirlooms loaned them for this occasion,—old vehicles, farming implements and everything that could represent the industries of Middletown in the olden time, or enhance the interest of the procession was pressed into service.

This city has from the earliest times been distinguished for her prominent men, who have occupied the highest position in all the walks of life—in the ministry, the law, medicine, science and business.

Middletown is now more attractive and desirable as a place of residence than ever before. The present activity in house-building is unprecedented in the annals of the city, nearly one hundred houses having been erected during the past year, and the carpenters are so hard pushed that it is difficult to secure their services.

Prominent streets have been newly paved and curbed. Two lines of horse-cars have been introduced, electricity is rapidly taking the place of gas, the water supply is very fine, and all the varied industries of the city are wakening to a broader and more active life under the influence of the electric spirit of the modern age.

LEADING BUSINESS MEN

OF

MIDDLETOWN.

Middletown National Bank, Middletown, Conn.—The banking interests and facilities of Middletown are not surpassed by those of any other community of equal size in the United States, and the Middletown National Bank is the oldest and has borne the most prominent part in the commercial history and life of the town. It was chartered as far back as 1795 and organized in 1801, but was reorganized under the national banking laws in 1865. Its best dividend, three dollars per share, was payable in July, 1882, and dividends of from six to twelve per cent per annum have continued up to date. In January 1890 the bank paid its tenth dividend, and it is but simple justice to say that during the entire ninety-five years of its existence it has been carried on in a manner which has won for it a brilliant record of unimpeachable honor, business stability and financial soundness of transaction, which reflects honor upon the community and the valuable and efficient services of its founders and proprietors. From first to last, many of Middletown's most successful and best known business men and manufacturers have been identified with this bank, and it is natural that an institution should prosper which conducted by those having an extended and thorough knowledge of the condition of affairs in the financial, industrial and commercial world, and being thoroughly identified with the advancement of the best interests of the section in which it is located. The president, Mr. M. B. Copeland, the vice president, Mr. E. K. Hubbard, and the cashier, Mr. Wm. H. Burrows, certainly need no introduction to our readers, and as they are associated on the board of directors with men equally prominent in the development of this section, it is not to be wondered at that the bank is everywhere looked upon as the representative financial institution of Middletown. A hint as to its financial condition is afforded by the fact that the surplus amounts to nearly one-half the capital stock, the latter being $300,000, while the surplus is $150,000. A general banking business is done and every facility is at hand to enable operations to be carried on to the best possible advantage, while the accounts of corporations, business firms, institutions and

individuals will be received on the most favorable terms, the management being liberal as well as wisely conservative.

Blake & Barton, Clothiers and Gents' Furnishers, 194 Main Street, Middletown, Conn.—Much of the prejudice that formerly existed regarding the wearing of ready made clothing has now passed away, and indeed there is no longer reason for its continuance, as ready made garments are now produced that are practically equal to the best custom clothing, and that are far superior to the "Middletown together" productions of cheap tailors with which the market is flooded. Of course ready made clothing is sold to-day that deserves all the ridicule that used to be cast at "slop shop" garments in general, but there is no necessity for any one being imposed upon through ignorance, for everybody has had an opportunity to inspect high grade ready made garments and hence should know what can be done in this line. The firm of Blake & Barton doing business at No. 194 Main street, has done good work in the past in educating the public up to a point where only the best of garments will prove acceptable, for it has never been satisfied to accept a second position, but has from the first maintained its place as a leader in the production of well-fitting, well made and fashionably cut clothing. Such has been the policy of Messrs. Blake & Barton since they founded their present establishment in 1887, and the result is to be seen to-day by the fact that their business has increased so rapidly that they have been compelled to move into much handsomer and more commodious quarters, and also on the high standing the firm have for probity, fair dealing and enterprise, in the best and truest sense of that much abused term. The enterprise of this firm does not consist of sharp dealing, and is not exemplified by its success in palming off clamed or superannuated goods on its customers in one presence or the other, but is shown in the low prices quoted on standard and fashionable clothing and gents' furnishings. Mr. W. C. Blake and Mr. H. L. Barton are both natives of Massachusetts, and are well known in Middletown as business men of established reputation.

F. A. Guild, Furniture Dealer and Undertaker. Agent for the "White Sewing Machine." Warerooms, 78 Main Street, Middletown, Conn.—Of the leading merchants on the Main street of Middletown none gain more prominence than the furniture warerooms of F. A. Guild, down

town. About three and one half years ago Mr. Guild opened this place with an entirely new and choice stock, showing remarkable taste in selecting the best and prettiest patterns that the market afforded and selling them at astonishingly low prices so that now he commands the largest trade in this city, doing last year more business than all the other furniture dealers in this city combined. Mr. Guild has been compelled to enlarge his ware rooms four times until now he occupies four large floors, 25 × 100 feet, and also the large basement at 84 Main street, 50 × 125 feet in dimensions, which he utilizes as upholstery and storage room for his surplus stock. Here you can find the White Sewing Machine, so well known for its light running and superiority over all other machines, which took the gold medal at the Paris Exposition as the best family sewing machine in the world, and here purchasers can look over and select with ease and convenience the furniture simple or elegant, plain and solid, or light and elaborately ornamented, which best suits their taste and the contents of their pocket books. Such an establishment as this is of great benefit to a town and thoroughly deserves the great and increasing patronage bestowed upon it. Mr. Guild also has a large upholstering and repairing department to his establishment, and is well known also as a funeral undertaker, because of his conscientious and faithful services and the abundant facilities ever at his command.

J. D. Sibley, Architect, 26 Church Street, Middletown, Conn.—The duties of an architect are varied and responsible, but they may be summed up in a very few words—the attainment of the best possible result under existing circumstances. Truly "circumstances alter cases," and in no profession are they to be more carefully considered than in that of architecture. The nature of the site, the comparative firmness and other characteristics of the soil, the appearance of surrounding buildings, the purposes for which the proposed structure is to be used, the amount of money which is to be put into it,—these and numerous other important points have to be considered by the successful architect, and the advantages gained by employing the services of such a man should most certainly be evident to every intelligent person. The magnitude of building operations in Middletown and vicinity makes this section a very promising field for a thoroughly competent architect, and Mr. J. D. Sibley, who has carried on operations here since 1875 finds a constant and increasing demand for his services. He is a native of New York State, and is extremely well known in this city, and was a member of the City Council in 1884-5. Mr. Sibley utilizes spacious office rooms at No. 26 Church street, and has two assistants to aid in the drawing up of plans, specifications, etc., so that such work can be done without undue delay. All business is assured immediate and painstaking attention, and those contemplating building would do well to give Mr. Sibley a call. He designed some of the most prominent buildings in this vicinity, and gives equally careful attention to the designing of public or business buildings and private residences, his charges being moderate in every instance. The residences of Henry E. Bullard and W. W. Wilcox, Jr., are notable instances of Mr. Sibley's work.

W. H. Chapman & Co., Saddlery Hardware, Sleigh Bells, Brass and Composition Castings, Middletown, Conn.—The manufacture of saddlery hardware is a great and growing industry and already has a heavy amount of capital invested in it, while it engages the attention of some of the most energetic and progressive business men of the country. Middletown is well represented in this as in many another field of effort, the establishment conducted by Messrs. W. H. Chapman & Co., being among the most extensive and most perfectly equipped of the kind in New England. The works cover an area of nearly two acres and include a very large three story building, besides various others of less importance. A very complete plant of machinery is operated, being furnished by a forty-horse engine. The firm began operations in 1826, the original partners being Messrs. W. H. and E. A. Chapman. Mr. E. Henry Barnes became associated with the concern in 1879, and in 1886 Mr. E. A. Chapman retired and Mr. George D. Chapman was admitted to partnership. All the gentlemen mentioned were born in this city, with the exception of Mr. Barnes, he being a native of New Haven. The members of the firm give close personal attention to the supervision of affairs, and the natural consequence is that orders are filled with a promptness and accuracy that have done much to commend the concern to the trade. Saddlery hardware, sleigh bells, brass and composition castings are very extensively manufactured, employment being given to seventy-five hands. The productions of this establishment are accepted as the standard wherever known, and as the firm are in a position to quote the lowest market rates it is hardly necessary to add that their business, large as it is, is steadily and rapidly increasing.

Goodyear Rubber Co., Middletown.—The manufacture of rubber goods has become one of the great industries of the country, and its future development gives promise of being practically unlimited, for new and useful applications of rubber are constantly being discovered, many of the articles made from this material are of such great utility as to be practically indispensable. At the head of the list must be placed rubber boots and shoes, for these are worn by everybody and millions of capital and thousands of people are engaged in their production. There is no article in the purchase of which the consumer is more absolutely dependent upon the reputation of the manufacturer to assure him that he is getting a fair equivalent for his money, for to the inexpert observer there is nothing to distinguish the good from the bad, and yet we all know from experience that some rubber boots and shoes will stand long and hard usage before wearing out, while others will crack and leak in a very short time. The only safe course to take then, is to ascertain what manufacturers make uniformly reliable goods and to insist upon having those and no others, and we may save our readers costly experimenting by recommending to them the boots and shoes, gold seal brand, made by the Goodyear Rubber Co. of Middletown, Conn. This company began operations here some eight years ago, and their goods have given such excellent satisfaction as to have built up an extensive and steadily increasing demand for them, the many orders received now requiring the employment of 150 hands and the utilization of a very complete and elaborate plant of machinery including an engine of 150 horse power. The premises made use of are 300 × 240 feet in dimensions, and are very conveniently arranged, the various processes incidental to production being carried on under the most favorable circumstances and every means being taken to reduce the cost of manufacture to the lowest figure consistent with the use of first class material and the maintenance of the enviable reputation now enjoyed by the product. Every honest dealer and every experienced consumer agree that "the best is the cheapest" where rubber goods are concerned, and those who make it a point to see that the trade mark of the "Goodyear Rubber Co." is stamped upon their purchases will find that they save both money and trouble by doing so.

The Russell Manufacturing Company, incorporated 1834. H. G. Hubbard, President; E. K. Hubbard, Vice-president; E. H. Burr, Treasurer; R. Mathewson, Secretary; R. L. Bailey, Agent, Middletown, Conn.—In compiling this necessarily brief account of the origin and development of the vast undertaking carried on by the Russell Manufacturing Company, we find ourselves in much the same dilemma as we would be were we required to pour a gallon into a half pint measure,—our intentions are excellent but our performance can hardly be a brilliant success—and yet as a review of Middletown's industrial enterprises containing no mention of this, the greatest of all, would be absolutely incomplete, we may be excused for making the trial. The Russell Manufacturing Company was incorporated in 1834 with a capital stock of $10,000, of which Messrs. Samuel Russell and Samuel D. Hubbard owned nine-tenths. A three story building, 30 y 80 feet in size was utilized, and the productions were confined to non-elastic web and suspenders. The predecessors of the company had failed and it looked for a time as if the disaster was to be repeated, for the company soon found themselves involved to the extent of $20,000 beyond their assets and the prospects were as dismal as they well could be. At this critical juncture, the Honorable Henry G. Hubbard (who had then barely attained his majority), was asked to take charge of affairs. He did so; bent all his energies to the task of familiarizing himself with the details of the business, and in 1841 brought out a power loom on which elastic web could be woven,—the first successful machine of the kind to be made, nor did he stop here. One improvement after the other was made, old methods were displaced by new and more efficient ones, no process of manufacture no matter how apparently trivial was allowed to escape notice, and the natural consequence was a steady gain in economy and accuracy of production which placed the company in a position to successfully meet all competition. Mr. Hubbard proceeded on the principle that to get business you must produce either better or cheaper goods than your competitors, and he succeeded in producing both. New productions were added from time to time, and to day the company manufactures a greater variety than any other similar concern in the world, among the leading productions being elastic web and suspenders, cotton and linen boot, gaiter and stay webs, cotton and worsted blanket bindings, halters and surcingles, patent cotton belting for machinery, patent hose goods for steam fire engines, together with seamless linen and cotton hose, patent cotton and hemp banding for mule harness, cotton yarn and thread, and linen hose for manufacturer's use. The manufacture of silk ribbons is a recent innovation and judging from the results thus far attained the venture is to prove a grand and permanent success. More than 5000 dozen suspenders are produced weekly, and of these and kindred goods over $1,000,000 worth is disposed of annually; the sales in the other departments exceeding $100,000. To turn out this immense product the services of more than 1000 assistants are required, together with the best equipped and most complete factories of the kind in the world, there being seven large mills operated, four of which are at South Farms one at Higganum, one at Rockfall and one at Staddle Hill. There are 20,000 spindles and 450 looms in constant use, the latter floating no less than 5000 shuttles. The spinning mills consume 5000 bales of cotton annually and turn out one and one-half million pounds of double and twisted yarn. Included in the plant are nine steam engines, seven water wheels, sixteen boilers, 100 cards and 100 sewing machines. Some of the belting is twenty inches wide and eight ply, giving it a thickness of half an inch. These figures convey some faint idea of the vastness of the business, but they fail utterly to give an adequate conception of the company's resources for these must truly be seen to be appreciated. They owe much of their efficiency to the fact that every department of the business is thoroughly systematized, one working in harmony with another, and all being conducted to the best advantage under the control of the man who made them what they

are to day—the Hon. Henry G. Hubbard. He has been the guiding spirit of the enterprise for more than half a century and during this time the capital has increased from $10,000 to $500,000, all of which great increase has come out of the profits of the business. Mr. Hubbard is a native of Middletown and has done much to advance her interests quite aside from the great influence his business enterprises have exerted in that direction. His career affords a shining example of what one man can do to benefit an entire community, and although but few may have his ability and opportunities, it should be remembered that his ability is largely the product of close observation and strict attention to the business in hand, and that his opportunities have been made and not waited for, for Mr. Hubbard has never followed the easy practice of "waiting for something to turn up," but has bent his energies to the task of utilizing existing conditions to the best possible advantage. Originally owning but a few shares of the company's stock he has increased his interest until now he holds so large a proportion of it as to be practically the company itself. He fills the position of president, and has associated with him Mr. E. K. Hubbard, as vice-president, Mr. E. H. Burr, as treasurer, Mr. Rufus Mathewson, as secretary and Mr. F. L. Bailey, as agent. The company have a store and office at Nos. 74 and 76 Worth street, New York, and distribute their productions throughout every portion of the Union.

The Rogers & Hubbard Company, Middletown, Conn.—Few have any idea of the great and varied utility of bone, for the average man looks upon this as a sort of waste product of little commercial value, but as a matter of fact bone is used in the manufacture of so many articles nowadays that were the supply suddenly cut off, great inconvenience would be the inevitable consequence, to speak in the very mildest terms. Middletown people naturally are better informed on this subject than the majority of their fellow men for in this town is located one of the most successful bone works in the United States, under the name of the Rogers & Hubbard Co., which began business in 1878. The original stock-holders were Maria E. Hubbard, W. F. Burrows, John Rogers, and Gaston T. Hubbard, but Mr. Rogers has disposed of his interest and F. Perry Hubbard, G. Tracy Hubbard and Ada H. Lindsay have become stockholders. All are natives of this town with the exception of Gaston T. Hubbard, and W. F. Burrows, the former having been born in North Carolina and the latter in Pennsylvania. The company's works cover about an acre of ground and are equipped with an elaborate plant of the most improved machinery, both water and steam being used as motive power. Some idea of the magnitude of the business may be gained from the fact that the bones of more than one million head of cattle are consumed annually, they being made into knife handles, buttons, druggists' goods and other articles, while the waste bone from the sawing department is utilized in the manufacture of fine fertilizers in which the company deals very extensively. The best case-hardening material in the market is also supplied by this company, and the enormous trade built up is the direct consequence of utilizing to the fullest extent what would otherwise be waste material,—the result of course being that the cost of production is reduced to a minimum and the company is consequently enabled to give the very lowest market rates. The fertilizers manufactured and sold by this concern are offered at much lower prices than would be possible were the company obliged to buy the bone, etc., used in their composition, and that the prices quoted on them are intelligently and not arbitrarily fixed is conclusively shown by the following guarantee, which it will be observed goes to the heart of the matter and disposes of certain oft quoted theoretical objections regarding official valuations in a most summary manner:

OUR GUARANTEE.—Any person buying our fertilizers, and upon having them analyzed, does not find the valuation equal to the price charged by us on board cars or boat, at Middletown, will upon sending us the analysis papers, of the Connecticut Agricultural Experiment Station with evidence to prove that samples were taken from full unbroken packages, receive from us a check for the amount of the difference.

THE ROGERS & HUBBARD CO.

The following is a list of the company's fertilizers: Pure ground raw knuckle bone flour, in bags of 167 pounds; strictly pure fine bone, in bags of 167 pounds; pure ground A N bone, in bags of 167 pounds. The Rogers & Hubbard Co.'s Complete Potato and Tobacco Manure, in bags of 200 pounds. Last year we placed this fertilizer on the market for the first time as a potato and tobacco manure of the highest order, free from chlorine and all other injurious or worthless elements. The experience of hundreds of practical farmers, has more than fulfilled our claims, and placed it at the head of all fertilizers for potatoes, tobacco and root crops. Fairchild's formula, for corn and general crops, in bags of 200 pounds. Another year's experience strengthens the confidence of the farmers in this fertilizer especially adapted to corn (all varieties), onions, cabbage, cauliflower, melons, tomatoes, beans, turnips, celery, top-dressing, and all general farm and garden crops. Fairchild's Formula for Oats, put up to order only. Oats can be raised at a profit without exhausting the land. Fairchild's Formula for Seeding Down, in bags of 200 pounds. A powerful, lasting fertilizer, made of raw knuckle bone and high grade muriate of potash, especially adapted to seeding down, with or without grain. It is unequalled for all varieties of wheat and rye, for restoring exhausted lands, for promoting the growth of apple, pear, peach, or ornamental trees, grape and berry vines. Stassfurt Muriate of Potash, 80 to 85%, in bags of about 225 pounds. Be sure your bags of muriate of potash are sealed with the lead tag of the syndicate. All muriate of potash in unsealed bags is of a low, inferior grade. Nitrate of soda, 97 to 99%, in bags of about 300 pounds; sulphate of potash, 90 to 98%, in bags of about 225 pounds; pure raw knuckle bone, "cattle flour," a clean sweet, white bone, resembling wheat flour in fineness and color. It is odorless and stock take it readily. No one can afford to winter their stock without it, as it promotes the general health of the herd especially that of the cows with calf. Cracked raw bone poultry feed, in any quantity desired. The great invigorating, health giving, egg-producing element in patent poultry food is the phosphate of lime derived from the bone used in its manufacture. Buy the pure article, 51% bone phosphate of lime. All orders will be promptly filled, and no pains spared to maintain the enviable reputation of the product in every respect.

Mrs. M. A. Smith, dealer in Dry Goods, Groceries, Boots, Shoes, Tinware, etc., South Farms, Middletown, Conn.—The establishment of Mrs. M A. Smith is a very extensive one of its kind, and the kind comprises such a vast stock of goods, articles of so varied a nature, that it is impossible to enumerate them in such limited space, and consequently difficult to do them justice. Mrs. Smith is a native of Middletown. The present house was established at South Farms, a suburb of Middletown, in 1870, and has as manager Mr. Joseph B. Phelps, who proves himself most efficient in this capacity. The inhabitants of South Farms and vicinity find it quite unnecessary to go to Middletown either for their large or small wants, though now that the horse cars, which connect the two places, run so conveniently, it is a comparatively short trip. Yet how troublesome even this is, when you can go into a store near by, and there find almost every necessity, food, clothing, household utensils, etc., etc. The business is retail solely, and occupies two floors of a building whose dimensions are 30 x 70 feet. This contains only a small part of the stock, and in addition Mrs Smith is obliged to have three store houses which are overflowing with all sorts of commodities. Five employées are kept busy attending to the brisk trade done in groceries, provisions, dry goods, boots, shoes, tinware, and the thousand and one things that are always needed in a household.

C. E. Jackson & Co., Bankers, Middletown, Conn.—Among those Middletown banking establishments in which the greatest confidence is reposed by the business public, prominent mention should in justice be made of the house of C. E. Jackson & Co., for since the inception of this enterprise its management has been of a character that very highly commends the undertaking to all appreciative of progressive and honorable methods and careful devotion to the interests of patrons. The firm is constituted of Mr. C E. Jackson and Dr A. W. Alsop, the latter gentleman being a special partner. Mr. Jackson is a native of Middletown and for more than twenty years has been treasurer of the Berkeley Divinity School. Since 1881 he has also filled the office of treasurer of the Russell Library. He was the first secretary of the Middlesex Banking Co and is now its vice president. Dr Alsop has served two terms as State Senator, and both gentlemen are very widely and favorably known in financial and social circles. The firm do a general banking business, taking deposits and buying and selling foreign exchange. They are one of the largest, if not the largest, dealers in high grade bonds in Connecticut, taking in the past ten years nearly all the large railroad and municipal loans issued in this State, and as a matter of fact this house placed the first four per cent railroad bond ever sold at par in the United States. The volume of business transacted requires the employment of five experienced assistants and the occupation of two spacious and well equipped apartments. With such facilities and so large a business experience it is no wonder that those wishing to increase their income, change the character of their investments, or dispose of property which it is necessary to turn into cash, will here find every facility to do so with expedition and security. Such an establishment as this is a decided public benefit, and fully deserves the cordial and continuous support of the business community.

Arrowwanoa Mills, I. E. Palmer, manufacturer of Cotton Tissues, Hammocks, Canopies and Canopy Fixtures; Crinoline Linings, Mosquito Netting, Window Screen Cloth, School Bags, Self-adjusting Pulleys, etc., etc. Sheer and Swiss Finishing a specialty, Middletown, Conn.—Among the many large manufacturing establishments in Middletown and vicinity there is not one more truly representative in its special line, or more interesting to visit, than that conducted by Mr. I. E. Palmer, and known as the Arrowwanoa Mills. These mills are advantageously located on Little River, and contain a very extensive and complete plant of improved machinery which is driven by water and a compound, condensing, steam-engine. Mr. Palmer is a native of Connecticut and has been identified with his present enterprise for many years, having begun operations in 1859. In 1868 the firm of Palmer & Kendall assumed possession, and after one other change the present proprietor resumed sole control in 1881. He is a very extensive manufacturer of cotton tissue, and makes a leading specialty of sheer and Swiss finishing. Among his most prominent productions may be mentioned hammocks, and in this specialty there is no other make that approaches "Palmer's Patent Hammock" in any particular, such as comfort, elegance or convenience. Crinoline linings, mosquito netting, window screen cloth and school bags are also largely manufactured, together with canopies and canopy fixtures, self adjusting pulleys, etc. All of these goods are favorably known to jobbers and the trade in general throughout the country. Mr. Palmer is in a position to fill the heaviest orders at comparatively short notice and to quote the lowest market rates on his various productions for his facilities are unsurpassed, and his long experience aids him materially in meeting all honorable competition. The Arrowwanoa Mills comprise five buildings, from two to four stories in height, and conveniently arranged as well as very thoroughly equipped. Employment is given to 100 operatives, and the careful supervision given every department of the business has its inevitable effect in the uniform superiority of the product.

W. & B. Douglas, manufacturer of Pumps, Hydraulic Rams, Garden and Fire Engines, Pump Chain and Fixtures, Well Curbs, Hydrants, etc., Middletown, Conn. (Branch Warehouses, 85 and 87 John Street, New York; and 197 Lake Street, Chicago, Ill.)—Middletown has her full share of those great manufacturing establishments which have made Connecticut famous throughout the civilized world, but it is safe to say that not one of them has done more to bring this about than that conducted by the firm whose card we print above. These works were founded by Messrs. William and Benjamin Douglas in 1832, and the present firm are not only the oldest but the most extensive manufacturers of pumps in the world, some idea of the magnitude of their business being afforded by the fact that their unabridged catalogue contains more than 1500 varieties and sizes of hydraulic machines, while the concern has a capital of $500,000 and utilizes a plant covering six acres and including three steam engines of 115 horse power, and the immense business is so thoroughly organized and so systematically conducted that every process is carried under skilful and careful supervision, and the consequence is that no imperfect work is allowed to leave the factory, so that dealers and users of pumps have learned to put entire confidence in every production of this famous firm. They have been awarded the highest medal at many competitions, prominent among them being those held at the Universal Exposition, Paris, France, in 1867, 1878 and 1889; Vienna, Austria, in 1873; Philadelphia, 1876; and Melbourne, Australia, 1881. The firm have modified and improved their styles from time to time, and having unequalled facilities, experience and capital it is not surprising that they should have attained results which place the Douglas pump beyond successful rivalry, it being conceded to have no equal for house, farm or factory use, either for hand or windmill power; hydraulic rams, garden and fire engines, pump chain and fixtures, well curbs, hydrants, etc., are all manufactured very extensively, and we need hardly say that Messrs. W. & B. Douglas are in a position to quote the lowest market rates on goods of uniformly superior quality and to fill the very heaviest orders at short notice. The firm maintain branch warehouses at Nos. 85 and 87 John Street, New York, and No. 197 Lake Street, Chicago, and their productions are not only shipped to every section of this country but a large foreign trade is also supplied. Mr. Benjamin Douglas, the president of the concern, has served several terms as Mayor of Middletown, and has also held the position of lieutenant governor. Mr. Benjamin Douglas Jr., acts as paymaster, and Mr. J. M. Douglas as secretary and treasurer, while the responsible positions of mechanical superintendent and assistant secretary were also filled by the late Edward Douglas, whose lamented death occurred in France, May 22, 1889. From first to last this enterprise has been of great direct benefit to Middletown, for it affords employment to many men and thus distributes large amounts of money, but its indirect benefit has been and is at least equally important, for this undertaking has made the city widely and favorably known and caused it to be respected by all who appreciate energetic and strictly honorable business methods.

Spain, O'Keefe & Co., Furniture Dealers and Undertakers, Warerooms 290 Main Street, Middletown, Conn. —It is a task of no small difficulty to select furniture, for there are so many styles to choose from and so many things to be considered before making a purchase that it is no wonder it is so hard for the average person to "make up his mind" as to just what he prefers. Of course if money is no object the matter is materially simplified, but unfortunately there are very few of us in that enviable position, and therefore the question of price is about the first one to be considered. Undoubtedly the most satisfactory mode of procedure is to visit an honorable dealer who has the reputation of quoting bottom figures, tell him what you want, how much you propose to spend, and thus give him an opportunity to judge intelligently as to what is best suited to your tastes and means. In our opinion no more satisfactory establishment can be visited than that conducted by Messrs. Spain, O'Keefe & Co., at No. 290 Main street, for a very desirable stock is there carried and a full dollar's worth of value is returned for every dollar paid out. This firm have had a wide experience in their present line of business and have built up a large trade by uniformly looking out for the interests of their patrons, considering them identical with their own and keeping good faith with every customer. Besides handling furniture, at the lowest market rates, a most important department of their business is that devoted to undertaking, a full assortment of caskets, coffins and other funeral goods being constantly on hand, and orders for undertaking in all its branches being assured immediate and painstaking attention, while the service rendered is of a character that cannot fail to give entire satisfaction to the most critical.

Henry Woodward, dealer in Drugs, Medicines, Chemicals, Paints, Oils, Acids and Dye Stuffs, 124 Main Street, Middletown, Conn.—This house is one of the largest as well as one of the oldest in this line in Middletown, as business was first commenced here in 1845 by Mr. George D. Howes, who was succeeded by Hubbard & Howes, which firm was followed by Mr. Charles H. Woodward, and in 1880 the business passed into the management of Mr. Henry Woodward of Middletown. Years of experience and good management have resulted in making the trade of this house the extensive and lucrative one which it is, and care has been not alone to carry and push, but also by a judicious and scrupulous adherence to the standard of perfect honesty which has been maintained from the outset. Drugs, medicines, chemicals, paints, oils, acids and dye stuffs are the articles handled. The extensive wholesale and retail business of this house require the assistance of numerous clerks. The premises are located at No. 124 Main street and comprise four floors, 88×20 feet each in dimensions, with one floor in storehouse 80×40 feet in dimensions. The stock of medicines will be found of the best quality and all the materials offered are of the first class and warranted to give satisfaction in every respect. Mr. Henry Woodward has held several official positions, which he has honorably filled, having been alderman, chairman of the State Fish Commission and trustee of Connecticut Hospital for the Insane. The retail department of this establishment will be found complete in every respect and full of everything required to constitute a first-class drug store.

Samuel T. Camp, dealer in Choice Family Groceries, Provisions, Flour, Meal, Wood and Willow Ware, etc., No. 138 Main Street, Middletown, Conn.—This house was established in 1858 under the name of Chaffee & Camp, but in 1867 Mr. Camp became sole proprietor of the business. Thirty-two years is quite a long period of time, and when a business enterprise has been conducted for such an extended term, and then stands higher than ever before in the estimation of its patrons, it is only fair to presume that it is due to genuine merit and reliability. Such is the record of which Mr. Camp's business can boast. The reason of this is to be found principally in the close and persistent personal attention which Mr. Camp has given to the undertaking, for there is a world of truth in the old saying: if you want a thing well done do it yourself. Mr. Camp is a native of Middletown and has been a member of the common council. The premises utilized are of the dimensions of 24×65 feet and comprise two floors well stocked with a finely selected assortment of groceries and provisions of all kinds. It is his aim to be able to meet any legitimate demand which may be made on a first-class establishment, and to attain this end he keeps his stock full in every department, and strives to supply goods at low market rates. Employment is given to six competent assistants to enable him to fill all orders promptly.

L. D. Brown & Son, manufacturers of Machine Twist and Sewing Silk. (Salesrooms, 486 Broadway, New York. 29 Lincoln Street, Boston, 1113 Market Street, Philadelphia.) Main Street, South Farms, Middletown, Conn.— The extensive establishment carried on under the firm name of L. D. Brown & Son on Main street, South Farms, Middletown, has been in operation since 1872, but the business of which it is a part is of much earlier origin, having been founded forty years ago by Mr. L. D. Brown, in Mansfield, Conn. This gentleman carried on operations alone from 1856 to 1862, when he took Mr. H. L. Brown into partnership under the firm name of L. D. Brown & Son, which is still retained, although Mr. H. L. Brown is now sole proprietor, having purchased his father's interest at the time of his death, in 1881. The founder of the enterprise was born in Coventry, Conn., and at one time was connected with the Mansfield board of selectmen. He was prominent in manufacturing circles and did much to improve the quality of American sewing silks. The present proprietor is a native of Mansfield, Conn., and has been connected with the Middletown municipal government for three years. The steadily increasing demand for the firm's productions shows that the high reputation of them has not suffered under the present management, and indeed it is an open secret that Mr. Brown spares no pains nor expense to keep the quality fully up to the highest standard, while at the same time quoting the lowest market rates on first class goods. The premises utilized for manufacturing purposes comprise a main building, three stories in height and 45×100 feet in dimensions; a dye house 30×60 feet in size, and a boiler room measuring 20×30 feet. The factory is equipped throughout with the latest improved machinery for the manufacture of machine twist, sewing silk, tram floss, tram, and all kinds of twisted silk. Employment is given to 150 experienced assistants, and all the many processes incidental to production are carried on under close and responsible supervision, the result being exceptional uniformity in the finished goods. The main characteristics of a first-class machine twist or sewing silk are smoothness, evenness of twist and coloring, and strength, and it is conceded that no goods in the market surpass the productions of Messrs. L. D. Brown & Son in any of these respects. Salesrooms are maintained at No. 486 Broadway, New York, No. 29 Lincoln street, Boston, and No. 1113 Market street, Philadelphia, a full assortment being carried at each of these points and manufacturers, jobbers and retailers being supplied in quantities to suit at the lowest market rates.

The Middlesex Banking Co. of Middletown, Conn. (Capital Stock, paid up, $600,000.)—In *Lippincott's Magazine* for March, 1890, is an article on Western mortgages which is deserving of very careful reading and which is as timely as it is instructive, for there is a very active demand at the present time for safe and profitable investments and the ideas contained in that article will enable any one of ordinary intelligence to discriminate properly between investment and speculation. After describing the difference between what are technically called Western mortgages and those made on property in the Eastern and Middle States, the writer says, referring to the former: "The investor has only one duty to perform, withal a very important one, viz., to determine once for all whether the company he is dealing with, by virtue of the character and ability of its officials, its established methods of business, the amount of its capital, and the availability of its assets, is able to give him a good and sufficient guarantee." The Middlesex Banking Company has from its organization in November, 1875, invited the most careful investigation of its financial standing and inquirers have been afforded all proper opportunities to gain a clear and comprehensive idea of just what the company's resources were and what might reasonably be expected of it in the future. As a consequence its business has steadily and rapidly developed, and now with a paid-up capital stock of $600,000 it stands higher than ever in the confidence of the investing public. The company's business is confined to dealing in first mortgage loans, these being made in Minnesota, North and South Dakota, Western Wisconsin, Texas and Colorado, through its general Western office at St. Paul, the managers of which are large stockholders in the company. These loans are marketed in the form of real estate first mortgage trustee debentures, bearing six per cent semi annual interest, in denominations of $100, $200, $250, $500, $1,000 and $5,000, due in seven, but redeemable after five years. The interest coupons are payable at the National Bank of the Republic, New York, the Broadway National Bank, Boston, the Girard Life Insurance, Annuity and Trust Co., Philadelphia, or at the banking house of the company in this city. As to the present standing of these debentures, after the company has been in business fifteen years, it is significant that in 1889 the Connecticut legislature passed a special act enabling holders of trust funds to invest in the debentures of the Middlesex Banking Company. The Union Trust Company of New York and the Security Company of Hartford are trustees for the Middlesex Banking Company, and the high standing of the enterprise is made even more apparent by the character of the gentlemen directly identified with it, as will be seen by a perusal of the following list: Robert N. Jackson, president; Merrick E. Vinton, first vice president; Charles E. Jackson, second vice president; William F. Graves, treasurer; D. T. Haines, secretary; Edw'd Holland Nicoll, assistant treasurer; E. A. Gladwin, assistant secretary. Trustees: Hon. Benj. Douglas, president W. & B. Douglas, Middletown; Thomas G. Carson, Boston; Russel Frisbie, J. & E. Stevens Co., Cromwell, Conn.; John M. Douglas, president Farmers & Mechanics Savings Bank; Robert N. Jackson, president; Merrick E. Vinton, Graves & Vinton Company, Saint Paul, Minn.; Charles E. Jackson, C. E. Jackson & Co., bankers, Middletown; William F. Graves, Graves & Vinton Company, Saint Paul, Minn.; Emory H. Nash, Pittsfield, Mass.; Austin R. Mitchell, president West Newton Savings Bank, West Newton, Mass. Graves & Vinton Company, Saint Paul, Minn., general Western managers.

E. H. Wells, Custom Tailor and Gents' Furnisher, No. 126 Main Street, Middletown, Conn.—No doubt many of our readers, especially those residing in Middletown, have already heard favorable reports of the custom tailoring establishment conducted by Mr. E. H. Wells, for those who do business with a house that is able to give perfect satisfaction both as regards its goods and its prices are very apt to communicate their experience to their friends so that they may take advantage of the same. The establishment in question was originally founded about 1858 by Messrs. Benham & Boardman, who were succeeded in 1866 by O. R. Benham, the present proprietor assuming control of affairs in 1884. Mr. Wells is prepared to do fine tailoring of every description, but caters especially to the best class of trade, paying particular attention to the cutting and fitting of both old and young men's garments, and producing fashionable clothing for their wear that in every detail will bear the severest comparison with that turned out at much more pretentious establishments. Two floors 20 × 60 feet in dimensions are occupied, and an extensive and varied assortment of gents' furnishings are carried, also a complete line of foreign and domestic fabrics are exhibited which will well repay careful inspection. Those who desire to dress with pleasing individuality will do well to remember that Mr. Wells makes a specialty of supplying suitings, etc., that are uncommon in design without being unpleasantly conspicuous, and a sufficiently varied assortment of styles is shown to allow all peculiarities of size and form to be provided for. The establishment is supplied with every facility for doing fine custom work. Sixteen skilled assistants are employed, and only experienced hands intrusted with the various details of making, etc., and under these circumstances Mr. Wells feels that he can confidently guarantee satisfaction, and warrant perfect fitting and durable garments.

Wm. Wilcox Manufacturing Co., manufacturers of Wrought Iron Plate and Padlocks, Wrought Iron French Rim Locks, and Wooden Hames, Middletown, Conn.—The business carried on by the William Wilcox manufacturing Company was founded nearly half a century ago, and its present magnitude is the legitimate result of the the thoroughly consistent policy which has characterized its management from the very first, for this policy has had the effect of giving the company's productions a most enviable and unsurpassed reputation for uniform merit. Operations were begun in 1845 and the existing company was incorporated thirty years later. Mr. William Wilcox, the president and treasurer, was born in Killingworth, Conn., and is one of the best known manufacturers in Middletown, he having held various local offices and having done much to develop the resources of the city and vicinity. The secretary, Mr. Clarence E. Atkins, was born in this city and has a large circle of friends throughout this section. The company is very extensively engaged in the manufacture of wrought iron plates and padlocks, wrought iron French rim locks, and wooden hames, and some idea of the magnitude of the business may be gained from the fact that the premises utilized cover an area of three acres. There are eight spacious buildings altogether, and with the exception of the foundries these each contain two floors. A very elaborate and complete plant of improved machinery is made use of, and about fifty horse water power is available, besides two steam engines of fifteen and twenty horse power respectively. Employment is given to ninety assistants, and the annual product is very large in amount and is readily disposed of, as the company's goods are shipped to all parts of the country and are accepted as the standard by consumers everywhere.

Levi S. Deming, dealer in Coal, Stone, Cement, and also Kindling Wood; Office and Yard, foot of William Street, Middletown, Conn.—The business now conducted by Mr. Levi S. Deming was founded many years ago by Mr. H. S. White, who was succeeded about 1860 by Messrs. White & Loveland, who gave place to Messrs. Loveland & Deming in 1871. In 1878 the firm name became White & Deming, and in 1887 the present proprietor (who is a native of Newington, Conn.) assumed sole control. The premises utilized comprise about one and one half acres and are located at the foot of William street, there being a river-frontage of 90 feet, and excellent facilities for the reception and the delivery of the various commodities dealt in, these including coal, stone, cement and kindling wood. Both a wholesale and retail business is done, and the employment of ten assistants enables all orders to be filled at the shortest possible notice. Mr. Deming handles all the most popular varieties of coal and makes a specialty of supplying family trade, furnishing clean and free-burning coal in large or small quantities at positively bottom prices. Kindling wood is another leading specialty at his establishment, and either hard or soft wood, sawed and split to suit, can be bought of him at remarkably low rates. He does a very extensive wholesale business also, furnishing a large proportion of the stone and cement used in this vicinity, and having the reputation of offering exceptional inducements to purchasers and thoroughly carrying out every agreement entered into.

Wm. Hall, dealer in cut Meats, Beef, Pork, Sausage, Lard, Hams, Poultry, etc., No. 42 East Court Street, Middletown, Conn.—One of the essentials to success in business in these days of close competition, is to thoroughly understand your particular line of trade in every detail, and there can be no doubt but that much of the popularity enjoyed by Mr. Wm. Hall at No. 42 East Court street, is due to the exceptional inducements he is enabled to offer, by reason of his perfect familiarity with the retail meat business, with which he has been identified for the past twenty-five years. He was born in Portland, Conn., and has carried on his present store since 1868. The premises are 18 x 60 feet in dimensions and are supplied with all necessary facilities for the storage and handling of a large stock of fresh and salt meats, including beef, mutton, pork, sausage, lard, hams, poultry, etc. Employment is given to two competent and polite assistants, and callers may depend upon receiving immediate and careful attention. Mr. Hall deals in first quality meats, and those who have found difficulty in getting cut meats to suit them would do well to place a trial order here, for the goods are the best that the market affords and the prices are uniformly moderate.

Middlesex County National Bank, Middletown, Conn. —The Middlesex County National Bank has long been recognized by well-informed business men as an exceptionally valuable institution through which to make financial dealings, its record being such as to place it prominent among the most progressive and reliable banks in the State. It was incorporated nearly sixty years ago, in 1831, and since its inauguration has continued uninterruptedly to transact its growing business in standing today an example of all that is best in the national banking system. The gentlemen identified with its management are looked upon as leaders in the mercantile and banking worlds, and by virtue of their long experience and high reputation as business men add both honor and influence to the prominent position occupied by this representative bank. One of the most potent factors in bringing about the present popularity and influence of the institution is the policy of conducting it in the interests of no one clique or branch of industry or commerce, but rather in the interests of all legitimate business enterprises. Its name, the "Middlesex County" National Bank, is not without peculiar significance for, as the business community have long since discovered, the policy of the management is broad enough to take in other interests besides those of Middletown alone, and the ability shown in carrying out this policy inspires confidence among all conversant with what has been done in the past, and gives ground for bright expectations of what may reasonably be anticipated in the future. Mr. G. W. Burr, the president, is one of the best known business men in this section of the State, and the cashier, Mr. Edwin P. Sheldon, is considered an authority on financial matters, and is especially popular among patrons of the bank from his willingness to accommodate them in all proper ways, although no man is a firmer believer in carrying on business on business principles, and no bank officer is more vigilant and untiring in protecting the interests of the institution with which he is identified. The Middlesex County National Bank has a capital of $250,000 and a surplus exceeding $65,000, being regarded by competent authority as one of the most absolutely solvent financial institutions in New England. It is consequently a most valuable bank to form connections with, and the high esteem in which it is held by other banks in different sections of the Union facilitates its business considerably and enables it to offer most efficient service in the collection of drafts and other duties incidental to the carrying on of a general banking business.

John Kincaid, manufacturer of and dealer in Harness, Blankets, Robes and Whips, Horse Furnishing Goods, etc., No. 162 Main Street, Middletown, Conn.—A harness, when on a horse, properly arranged, etc., is a very simple thing in appearance, and apparently is made up of but few parts, but the same harness when divided up into all the pieces that are combined in its construction, has a very different aspect, and no one can examine it then without feeling that after all, harness making is not the easy thing it may appear to be, considering the cost of the material, and the labor involved in making it up. A first-class harness is sold at a very reasonable figure, and although it is possible to find establishments where fancy figures are charged, still on the whole, most people would prefer to place their orders with such a house as that of Mr. John Kincaid, and thus assure themselves a superior article and uniformly fair treatment. This gentleman has carried on his present enterprise since 1885, and has gained a well-earned reputation for the manufacturing of fine harness and the maintenance of moderate rates. Mr. Kincaid is a native of Hartford, Conn., and is well known throughout Middletown. The premises utilized measure 15 x 85 feet, located at No. 162 Main street, and light and heavy harness of every description are manufactured. Repairing and custom work of all kinds is neatly and promptly done. Mr. Kincaid also deals extensively in blankets, robes, whips, etc., and horse furnishings in general are carried in stock and offered at very low prices.

J. W. HUBBARD & CO.,

DEALERS IN

Lumber, Nails, Lath, Lime, Cement, Hair, etc.

Mouldings, Wood Turning.

Scroll Sawing and Stair Building.

Hanover St. **MIDDLETOWN, CONN.**

The firm of J. W. Hubbard & Co. began business in 1877. Since that time they have built up a large and increasing trade in lumber, nails, lath, lime, cement, hair, etc., and utilize premises having an area of about two acres, located upon Hanover street. Mouldings and other house finishings are also largely handled, while wood turning, scroll sawing and stair-building will be done quickly and at moderate rates. The members of the firm are Messrs. J. W. and W. E. Hubbard, both of whom are natives of this city.

O. S. Watrous, D. D. S., and Associate Dentists, 159 Main Street, Middletown, Conn.—At 159 Main street, Middletown, may be found the most complete dental office in Middlesex county, with all the most recent improvements in dental appliances among which is a specially constructed furnace for baking porcelain, with which Dr. Watrous and his four associates are enabled to construct the teeth for special cases. They make a specialty also of artificial teeth without plates, for which they hold the exclusive license for this county. Difficult cases in all branches of the profession are solicited. Besides having a large practice in Middletown and vicinity, very many of Dr. Watrous' patients come from New York and other distant places, that they may be under his skillful care and it is almost always necessary to apply long in advance to secure a sitting, so completely is his time engaged. Facts speak for themselves, and those whose teeth have once been under Dr. Watrous' care are very rarely willing to go elsewhere.

D. L. Weeks & Son, wholesale and retail dealers in Crockery, China, Glass and Earthen Ware, Lamps, Brackets, Chandeliers, Silver-Plated Ware, etc., No. 210 Main Street, Middletown, Conn.—A very attractive establishment to housekeepers is the one kept by D. L. Weeks & Son at 210 Main street. Mr. H. E. Weeks, since the death of his father the sole proprietor, is a native of Greenpoint, L. I., coming to Middletown in 1865, he has for many years been identified with the business interests of Middletown. He takes just pride in the welfare of the city and is at present a member of the town council. He does an extensive trade, both wholesale and retail, and occupies extensive premises at 210 Main street, which comprises two floors and cover an area of 25 x 75 feet. In addition to this building he has a large store house of 40 x 150 feet dimensions. The stock comprises crockery of all grades, from the finest foreign and American china to the ordinary earthenware vessels, which are so useful and not by any means to be despised on account of their lack of beauty. Glass, which adds so much to the attractiveness of a table, is to be found here to suit all purses—also a great variety of the famous Rochester lamps, brackets and other useful and necessary household articles. In addition to this, Mr. Weeks keeps a line of silver-plated ware, forks, spoons, etc., etc. The stock is an extensive and complete one and Mr. Weeks strives to offer the best articles at as low prices as is possible. This is easy to discover by paying a visit to his establishment, where he and his three assistants are always in readiness to show every politeness to their customers.

Farmers and Mechanics Savings Bank. Incorporated 1858. Middletown, Conn.—In a history of the origin and development of the more important commercial enterprises of a community, great prominence must of course be given to the banking institutions carried on therein, for on these are dependent in a great measure the solvency and financial power of the people. Especially is this true of those designed for the reception of savings, and the best possible indicator of the condition of trade and of the habits of the inhabitants of any section, is that afforded by the reports of such institutions. Savings banks are now looked upon by the most enlightened political economists as being at least as valuable in the conservation of order as an equal number of police stations and certainly the direct and powerful influence they exert in inculcating habits of industry and prudence among the people is worthy of careful consideration in summing up the saving elements in a community. But a savings bank, to be worthy of the name, must possess in the highest degree the respect and confidence of the people and it is just such an institution of which we propose to make record here. We refer to the Farmers and Mechanics Savings Bank, which, since its organization in 1858, has by the ability and enlightened conservatism shown in its management, come to be regarded as financially solid almost as the nation itself. Those conducting it are recognized as representative citizens all over the State, among them being John M. Douglas, who acts as president, and Samuel T. Camp as vice-president, and Fred B. Chaffee, who officiates as secretary and treasurer. All these gentlemen were born in Middletown, and Mr. Douglas has held various local offices besides serving as State senator, Mr. Camp being a successful merchant. The board of directors is composed of the following gentlemen well known in the community and State: E. Bound Chaffee, Samuel Stearns, Jr., O. Vincent Coffin, Alfred Cornwell, Dr. Leonard Bailey, Arthur B. Calef, Geo. T. Meech. By a recent computation it was shown that the securities held by the bank have been so judiciously selected as to have a market value nearly $78,000 in excess of their par value. This bank can pay its depositors in full and have surplus $170,000, and this is but one of many things going to show that every dollar deposited in the Farmers and Mechanics Savings Bank is as safe as it well can be.

D. L. Briggs & Co., dealers in Chicago Dressed Beef, Lamb, Mutton, Pork, Lard Hams, etc.; office, Old Branch Passenger Depot, Middletown, Conn.—The residents of this country have been characterized as "a nation of meat eaters," and every American probably knows that we do in fact consume an enormous amount of meat *per capita* when the entire consumption is equally divided among the population, but in order to really appreciate to some degree the actual amount required to supply even a single section of the country, one should visit some such establishment as that conducted by Messrs. D. L. Briggs & Co., in the old branch passenger depot. This firm do an exclusively wholesale business and deal in Chicago dressed beef, lamb, mutton, pork, lard, hams, etc., supplying many prominent retailers throughout this vicinity. They receive beef and other meats literally by the ton, for the premises are so arranged as to admit car-load lots, car and all, and the first question that comes into the mind of the casual visitor is "What in the world can they do with all this meat?" The firm had no difficulty in disposing of it, however, for first class meats sell readily in this section and Messrs. D. L. Briggs & Co. are prepared to supply goods that will suit the most fastidious. Their storage facilities are on a par with the other conveniences noticeable, the cold storage room having an area of no less than 1800 square feet. Orders are promptly filled with the aid of five assistants, and the lowest market rates are quoted on all the various commodities handled. This representative firm is made up of Messrs. D. L. Briggs and A. J. Briggs, both of whom are natives of Sackville, N. B., and need no personal introduction to our Middletown readers, especially the senior partner, for he served on the board of aldermen during the years 1888 and 1889, and is now mayor of the city.

G. M. Southmayd, Undertaker. A full line of goods used in the business constantly on hand. Marble Burial Vaults. Also agent for The White Bronze Monuments in Middlesex County. No. 266 Main Street, Middletown, Conn.—That Mr. G. M. Southmayd is one of the best known funeral undertakers in the city, must be evident to all who are at all familiar with the magnitude of his business for his long and varied experience is availed of by a very large circle of customers and his facilities, ample as they are are not in frequently severely taxed to meet the heavy demands made upon them. Mr. G. M. Southmayd is a native of Middletown and has carried on his business since 1865, having at that date succeeded Mr. John B. Southmayd, who founded this undertaking in 1845. His present establishment is located at No. 266 Main street, and comprises two floors of the building, each 21x60 feet in dimensions, and is complete in every department. Employment is given to four efficient assistants and a full line of goods used in the business is constantly on hand. Mr. Southmayd is agent for the White Bronze Monuments in Middlesex county. He has a fine assortment of coffins, caskets, and slate burial vaults, as well as grave clothes of various styles and qualities, and is prepared to assume entire charge of funerals, and everything will be furnished in first-class style at very moderate rates. Mr. Southmayd is very much respected and esteemed in the community, and is fully deserving of the good wishes so often bestowed upon him. He served in the army as captain of Co. A, 11th Regiment, and held the office of councilman for 1870-71-72; alderman for 1884, and State Representative for 1886.

Geo. G. Thayer, dealer in Groceries, Provisions and Fruits, also a Good Line of Crockery and Glass Ware. 60 Main Street, Middletown, Conn.—There is no kind of business enterprise that is more popular, when it is carried on in the proper manner than that of the grocer and provision dealer, and the reason is obvious, for there is no line of business in which the proprietors enter into more close relations with their customers. Take the establishment conducted by Mr. Geo. G. Thayer for an example. The enterprise was inaugurated 1880 by its present proprietor and has steadily grown in patronage and appreciation, until now it ranks among the first-class establishments of Middletown. Mr. Thayer is a native of New York State and has a large number of friends in this vicinity. The premises utilized are 18x60 feet in size and contain a heavy stock, for Mr. Thayer does an extensive retail business, and deals in a great variety of articles. Choice groceries, fresh provisions and fruits are handled, especial advantages being offered in these lines of superior goods, at bottom prices. This establishment is located at No. 60 Main street, where all goods dealt in are sold in quantities to suit. Crockery and glass-ware are also dealt in and the variety offered is sufficiently great to allow of all tastes being suited. Two reliable assistants are employed, orders are promptly filled and fair dealing is assured to all.

The Middletown Savings Bank, Incorporated A. D. 1825, George A. Coles, President, Henry H. Smith, Treasurer. Middletown, Conn.—The capacity to save money is of almost equal importance to the capacity to earn it, and indeed we are by no means sure but that the one is the peer of the other, for what every young man should learn is that it is not what is earned but what is saved that constitutes wealth. The first step towards inducing people to save a portion of their earnings is to provide a place for their deposit where they may feel a moral certainty that all is safe and secure, and then if a certain percentage be allowed them for the use of their funds, more than half the battle is won. It is just such a noble work as this that has been accomplished by the founder of the Middletown Savings Bank and their successors, and it would be difficult indeed to overestimate the good that has been wrought in the community by their means. Over sixty-five years ago the original charter of this institution was granted, it being issued in 1825, when there were less than a dozen similar enterprises in the entire country. At the present time savings banks are numbered by the hundreds; they are to be found in every town of any importance throughout the Eastern and Middle States, while many are located in the West and South, and they exercise a stimulating and yet conservative influence which make them a mighty power for good, and which goes farther to assure a peaceable and reasonable settlement of the industrial and social questions of the day than any other influence that can be named. And it should never be forgotten that it is mainly to the ability and integrity of the managers of the pioneer institutions, prominent among them being the Middletown Savings Bank—that this rapid and continuous development is due, for " by their fruits ye shall know them," and had the first savings banks proved failures it would have been many years before the confidence of the people could have been restored. The Middletown Savings Bank has steadily gained in public favor and support until now it has in its custody deposits approximating five and a half millions of dollars. This enormous sum is safely and profitably invested, and depositors are given a liberal rate of interest, while the conservatism of the management is attested by the existence of a surplus of very nearly $800,000. Mr. George A. Coles is president of the bank, and Mr. H. H. Smith treasurer, while the board of trustees is made up of representative business men who possess to an exceptional degree the esteem and confidence of the community.

G. E. Burr, dealer in Fancy and Family Groceries, Flour, Meal, Wood and Willow Ware, Foreign and Domestic Fruits, No. 89 Main Street, Middletown, Conn.—It is by catering especially to family trade that Mr. G. E. Burr, who is engaged in the sale of fancy and family groceries, has worked up the very liberal patronage he now enjoys, and no one who has observed the methods by which his establishment has been advanced to its present prominence, can begrudge him the success attained, for it has been won, not by belittling competitors and seeking to injure any man, but by conscientious, intelligent and untiring work of the hardest kind. Mr. G. E. Burr was born in Middletown, and founded his present business under the name of Burr Brothers, and since 1880, has had entire control and management of affairs. He now occupies premises located at No. 89 Main street, comprising a store 18 x 100 feet in dimensions, also a store room 12 x 18 feet, and the services of four competent assistants are required to enable him to fill all orders with celerity and accuracy. The stock on hand is a very full and varied one, including as it does fancy and family groceries, flour, meal, wood and willow ware; also foreign and domestic fruits of all kinds. Mr. Burr has reason to take special pride in the goods furnished to patrons, for it is often remarked among those who have tested them, that their equal is very hard to find elsewhere for the money. The prices are reasonable in every department, and customers of this house can depend on getting a fair equivalent for their money every time.

Walter H. Smith, Hack, Livery, Boarding and Sale Stable. Carriages for Parties, Funerals, etc. Best Ladies' and Gentlemen's Single and Double Driving Teams in the City. Stable Open Day and Night. Telephone Connections No. 33 East Court Street, Middletown, Conn.—There are some people who think that every dollar spent for anything beside the actual necessities of life is wasted, but happily these people are becoming fewer in number every year, and the great majority of the public are firm believers in the motto " All work and no joy makes Jack a dull boy," or in other words, as the world grows wiser it appreciates the fact that recreation is as important, and as necessary to the maintenance of health as food or shelter. No more healthful and enjoyable recreation than driving has yet been discovered, and we are perfectly convinced that if some of our readers would spend less money for drugs and doctor's bills, and taste for horse-hire, they would be heartier and happier in every way. A good horse, an easy carriage and a pleasant road combine to make a more valuable recipe for the preservation or regaining of health than two-thirds of the doctor's prescriptions, and certainly this recipe is " easier to take " than any drug. You can get all its ingredients but the road at the hack, livery, boarding and sale stable conducted by Mr. Walter H. Smith, at No. 33 East Court street, and our readers need not be told that there is no lack of good roads and pleasant drives in Middletown and vicinity. Many competent judges agree that Mr. Smith furnishes the best ladies' and gentlemen's single and double driving teams in the city, and no one denies that his accommodations are unsurpassed while his prices are as low as those quoted at any other first-class Middletown stable. Spacious and well equipped premises are occupied and employment is given to seven assistants, every order being assured immediate and careful attention. The stable is open day and night, and has telephone connections. Carriages will be furnished for parties, weddings, funerals, etc, and moderate charges are made in every instance. Mr. Smith is a native of Rocky Hill, Conn, and served as State Representative during 1879-80. He has carried on his present enterprise since 1883, and his business is not only large but steadily and rapidly developing.

Charles A. Bailey, Designer and Sculptor, Die Sinking, Model Making, Modeling of Ornamental Patterns, Engraving, Steel Hubs Cut, and Model Making to Order. Machinery designed for performing Special Operations, or making New Articles. 140 Main Street (up stairs), Middletown, Conn.—It is obvious that a designer and sculptor must be capable of producing the most accurate work if he is to be successful, and the results attained at the establishment of Mr. Charles A. Bailey, No. 140 Main street, up stairs, have been such as to entitle him to rank among the most skillful and reliable designers and sculptors in this section. Mr. Bailey is a native of Chatham, Conn., and began operations here in 1880. His premises are well equipped, and he is consequently able to fill orders at short notice, as well as to guarantee satisfaction as regards the character of the work. Die sinking, mould making, modelling of ornamental patterns, engraving, steel hubs cut, and model making is done to order, and low charges are made in every department. Machinery is designed for performing special operations or for making new articles. Special attention is given to the modeling of portraits from photographs, and produced in bronze, a good likeness being guaranteed, and those wishing anything of the kind done, would best serve their own interests by giving Mr. Bailey a call before placing their orders elsewhere. He is a skillful and experienced designer and has a reputation as an inventor, and all business entrusted to him will be kept strictly private. He can readily understand and put into shape devices that would puzzle those less perfectly equipped. The very finest work is put into his productions, and we feel that all who may patronize Mr. Bailey will have no reason to regret having done so.

D. R. Brownlow, dealer in Groceries, Provisions and Variety Goods, Stoves, Tinware and Plumbing, Steam and Gas Fitting, 12 Warwick Street, Middletown, Conn.—Mr. D. R. Brownlow was born in Middletown, and inaugurated his present enterprise in 1865, having thus been identified with it, for a quarter of a century. He has gradually increased the scope and the magnitude of his business until it has become one of the leading enterprises of the kind in this section. It is located at No. 12 Warwick street, and occupies spacious quarters, there being two floors each 20 × 40 feet, with an extension 15 × 26 feet. A very large and valuable stock is constantly carried, and so varied is it that lack of space renders detailed mention impossible, but suffice it to say that you can find about anything in the line of groceries, provisions and variety goods, here, and we may add that you will also find that the prices are in every instance as low as the lowest, quality considered. An important department of the business is that devoted to the handling of stoves, tinware, etc., a full assortment of the best makes being constantly carried in stock. Mr. Brownlow is also a practical plumber, steam and gas fitter, and as employment is given to ten competent assistants, orders in any branch of the business will receive prompt attention, and will be filled in the most satisfactory manner. Mr. Brownlow is a native of Middletown, and was councilman several years previous to 1884, and was a member of the water board for 1884, 1885, 1886 and 1887.

W. A. Brower, Commission Broker; Stocks, Bonds, Grain and Provisions. Telephone and Private Wire. Correspondent Doran & Wright Co., New York. No. 157 Main Street, Middletown, Conn.—The establishment conducted by Mr. W. A. Brower, at No. 157 Main street, is worthy of particularly prominent and favorable mention in a review of Middletown's mercantile and industrial enterprises, first because it is the only one of the kind in the city, and second because the facilities offered are exceptionally complete and reliable. Mr. Brower is a native of New York City, and began operations in Middletown in 1887. He has built up an extensive and steadily increasing business, and gained an enviable reputation for ability and integrity. He is a commission broker in stocks, bonds, grain and provisions, and his office has direct communication with the great trade centres by telephone and private wire, the latest quotations being received and all necessary information being furnished to allow large or small investments to be intelligently made. Mr. Brower is correspondent of the Doran & Wright Company of New York, and business may be transacted through him with as much dispatch and reliability as though the investor were at the home office of that representative concern.

Frank E. Willis, Photographer, studio, 158 Main Street, Middletown, Conn. The day when it was necessary to pay an exorbitant price for a photograph has passed, and there is now no reason why everybody should not possess an artistic portrait. There is no need to enter into an argument to uphold our position so far as the Middletown people are concerned for all they have to do is to call on Mr. Frank E. Willis at No. 158 Main street, and see what he has to offer as regards goods and prices. The illustrations in this book are from photographs obtained at his studio. We also understand that he always has for sale a fine assortment of views of all the principal points of interest in Middletown and vicinity. Mr. Willis is a native of Keene, N. H., and succeeded Mr. F. J. Moore in business in 1889. The premises utilized comprise a large and pleasant reception room, operating room and work room. He is steadily increasing the number of his patrons by strict attention to business, good work and fair prices, and honorable dealing and deserves the cordial support and appreciation of this vicinity. Mr. Willis and his two assistants are always ready and willing to give prompt and polite attention to all patrons.

D. I. Chapman, dealer in Choice Groceries, Provisions, Fruit and Vegetables, No. 88 Main Street, Middletown, Conn.—The briskness and energy manifested in the enterprise carried on by Mr. D. I. Chapman, are in refreshing contrast to the methods pursued at some other establishments of a similar nature, and it is not to be wondered at that a large business has already been built up, although the undertaking was not inaugurated until 1886, premises measuring 20 × 40 feet, and located at No. 88 Main street are made use of, and the stock of choice groceries on hand is so varied and complete that all tastes can be suited and all orders filled without delay. Provisions of all kinds are also very extensively dealt in, and fruit and vegetables in great variety in their seasons, and the prices quoted on all goods handled are quite enough to explain his popularity with housekeepers. Mr. Chapman was born in Ledyard, Conn., and is well known among our business men. He employs three efficient and accommodating assistants, and customers are attended to at once; orders being promptly and accurately delivered. Mr. Chapman gives close personal attention to the various departments of his business.

C. A. Pelton, wholesale and Retail Druggist. Proprietor of the Celebrated American Cough Drops, Dr. Griffith's Plaster, Collin's Kallocrine or Medicated Hair Tonic, and Pelton's Stomach Bitters. 52 Main Street, Corner William, Middletown, Conn.—Few establishments in New England, or, in fact, in the whole country, can boast of a longer standing than the present house of Mr. C. A. Pelton. With just pride many say "I have been in my business twenty years." But how many men can boast of being the owner of a house which began with the century, and has been doing a flourishing trade for ninety years! Mr. Pelton is a native of Middletown. He is a wholesale and retail druggist and the present representative of the house founded in 1800. Mr. E. C. Hubbard was the proprietor in 1851, Mr. Pelton becoming his clerk in 1855. Eleven years later, 1862, the business changed hands, Mr. Pelton becoming part owner with Mr. Collins, and the firm was known as Collins & Pelton. The name was again changed in 1871, when Mr. Pelton became sole proprietor, which position he has held ever since, proving himself eminently efficient in carrying on this important branch of industry. The premises at 52 Main street occupy three floors, each of the dimensions 20×85 feet, and three assistants are employed to attend to the many duties of a druggist's business. Besides the ordinary line of trade, putting up prescriptions, which is of course, the most important branch, Mr. Pelton is proprietor of the celebrated American Cough Drops, so efficacious for any bronchial trouble, for Dr. Griffith's plaster, and Collin's kallocrine or medicated hair tonic, very useful for invigorating the hair or to prevent its falling. Besides being well known as a business man, Mr. Pelton has had four terms of public service, having been a member of the city council in 1868-9 and 1871-2.

Wm. B. Davis, Grocer, Provisions, etc. Choice Line of Fruits and Vegetables Always on Hand. Tobacco and Cigars. No. 62 Main Street, Middletown, Conn.—Residents of Middletown certainly do not suffer from a lack of grocery and provision stores, for there are a number of these needful establishments in the vicinity in proportion to the population. But this is a case where the right sort of it is a fault at all, for "competition is the life of trade," and here energetic men with genuine above undue competition as long as reputable methods are adhered to. We are sure that Mr. Wm. B. Davis of No. 62 Main street, has no fault to find, at all events, and indeed it would be surprising if he had, as his trade is large as it is, and is constantly increasing. Mr. Davis succeeded Mr. N. G. ... in business in ... and has been sole proprietor since that date. ...

Lyman Payne, dealer in Pianos and Organs and General Musical Merchandise. Agent for the Decker Brothers, Hallet & Cumston, and Newby and Evans Pianos, and the Estey and Loring & Blake Organs. Instruments Rented and Sold on Installments, or at Very Low Prices for Cash. No. 167 Main Street, Middletown, Conn.— "Music hath charms to soothe the savage breast," no doubt, but it hath charms to accomplish a still more satisfactory result—make home what it should be, the pleasantest spot on earth. Anything that will promote good feeling in the domestic circle is to be encouraged, and certainly nothing is more valuable in this respect than music ...

Hennigar Bros., Photographers, Rooms 136 Main Street, Middletown, Conn—There are not a few people who think it necessary to visit the largest cities in order to obtain a first class portrait, and who would laugh at the the idea of being able to get an equally faithful and handsomely finished likeness at home, yet expert photographers are not confined to the more important cities by any means, and we have an instance of this in the firm of Hennigar Brothers, whose popular studio is located at No. 136 Main street. This photographic establishment was founded by Mr. G. W. Hennigar in 1861, and the generous patronage bestowed upon him showed that his work was equal to any in this vicinity. In 1890 the firm-name was

Lyman D. Mills, dealer in Stoves and Tin ware, Plumbing, Tin Roofing, Steam and Hot Water Heating and Gas Fitting. No. 16 East Court street, Middletown, Conn.—Since the enterprise now conducted by Mr. Lyman D. Mills was inaugurated in 18..., many and varied improvements have been made in methods and heating stoves and methods of doing business ...

George M. Pratt (Successor to Artis Hyde) dealer in Coal and Wood, Office foot of Court Street, Connected by Telephone, Middletown, Conn.—There is an immense amount of coal and wood disposed of annually in Middletown and vicinity, and we think it would surprise many of our readers to learn the average consumption of these commodities per week, and the magnitude of the business in both its wholesale and retail departments. Among local dealers in coal and wood it is perfectly safe to say that not one bears a higher reputation than does Mr. George M. Pratt who succeeded Mr. Artis Hyde in 1886. ...

IRA L. GARDINER, Agent for the CELEBRATED WALTER A. WOOD MOWER, REAPER AND HORSE RAKE.

Produce and Commission Merchant. Dealer in Bananas, Oranges, Lemons, Figs, Grapes, Nuts, etc. Walter A. Wood's Mowing Machines and Horse Rakes, Plows and Repairs for same. 121 Main Street, Middletown, Conn.— Among the numerous business men who do a thriving trade in Middletown is Mr. Ira L. Gardiner. He is well known by the inhabitants as being one of the first produce and commission merchants of the place, not only for the quality of his goods, but for the many years he has been established among them. Born and brought up in Middletown, Mr. Gardiner chose his native place as the scene of his business efforts. These he began as far back as 1853, his trade which is both wholesale and retail growing steadily with the growth of the town. He makes a specialty of agricultural implements and has been agent for many years of the celebrated Walter A. Wood mower, reaper and horse-rake, which has just received the first prizes at the Paris exposition. Farmers will find here a wealth of other articles necessary for their pursuits. Among these may be mentioned Blanchard churns, Fyler churns, grass seeds, hay cutters, Centennial swivel plow, Oak chilled plow, Wyard's sulky plow, Gray's horse powers and repairs for same. Many varieties of fertilizers are also kept in stock, H. J. Baker & Bros.' fertilizers, phosphates, ground bone, ground plaster—potash salts, and Worcester brand of salt. This house is also agent for the Hitchcock potato digger, which is a favorite with so many farmers. Mr. Gardiner's career has not been solely a business one. As alderman he has served three terms and at the present time he is filling the office of selectman.

Benj. F. Turner, dealer in Groceries, Provisions, Flour and Feed, Durham Avenue, Middletown, Conn.—In one sense of the word, practically all retail grocery and provision stores are alike, but it will be found on more intimate acquaintance that stores differ as much as people do, and the more thoroughly you are acquainted with them the more broad the difference appears. Every establishment has distinguishing characteristics of its own, and perhaps the most prominent feature of the store carried on by Mr. Benj. F. Turner, on Durham avenue, is the dependence that can safely be placed upon all representations made there. This establishment was founded by Mr. James F. Turner in 1855, and the firm-name has since been changed to its present style, Benj. F. Turner. Mr. Turner is a native of Middletown. Three well informed assistants are employed, and an extensive retail trade has been built up in choice family groceries, provisions, flour, feed, etc. Mr. Turner's goods are always satisfactory and his prices equally so. He carries an exceptionally heavy stock, utilizing premises comprising a store and basement each 30 x 80 feet in dimensions, in addition to a storehouse comprising two floors, each 20 x 20 feet in size. He makes it a rule to keep his assortment complete in every department, and there are few articles coming under the head of choice family groceries and provisions not handled by him. Prompt and polite attention is assured to all

Frank D. Brewster, manufacturer of and dealer in Men's and Boys' Custom and Ready-Made Clothing, Cloths and Furnishing Goods, 106 Main Street, Corner College Street, Middletown, Conn.—One of the most useful establishments possible in a community, is such as is conducted by Mr. Brewster on Main street. His goods are not only indispensable in kind, but fine in quality and low in price, therefore it is only natural that his trade should be a large and increasing one. Those wishing anything in the line of ready-made clothing will find it to their advantage to visit this store. If a customer prefers to have his clothing made to order, Mr. Brewster is also ready to accommodate him, as he carries a fine selection of cloths and furnishing goods from which you can take your choice, and he is a manufacturer as well as a dealer in men's and boys' clothing. He keeps constantly on hand a full assortment of everything in this line. This house was established in 1860 by Mr. Charles E. Benham and after several changes in the management Mr. Frank D. Brewster became sole proprietor in 1870. The premises are located at the corner of Main and College streets, and the space occupied measures 25 x 65 feet. Employment is given to two competent assistants, and the assortment shown of fashionable and thoroughly made garments should certainly be seen before purchasing elsewhere. Suits are on hand designed for either dress or business wear, and some styles are designed for both purposes, and are elegant and correct at all times. The newest styles and patterns will be found in each department and low prices will prevail. All orders are accurately attended to, and all business is transacted in an honorable and satisfactory manner.

Parshley & Co., dealers in Fine Hats, Shoes and Gents' Furnishings, No. 72 Main Street, Middletown, Conn.— People who dress the best are those who most thoroughly realize the fact that one's appearance depends more upon the accessories than the main portion of the costume, or in other words, that it is easy to maintain a neat and fashionable appearance at but comparatively small expense by using care and judgment in the selection of hats, boots, neckwear, etc. But few really appreciate this fact, but it is a fact, and one well worth bearing in mind, for by taking advantage of it money can be saved and very satisfactory results attained. Of course it is necessary to use judgment in order to buy hats, shoes, furnishings, etc., to the best advantage; but this is easily done by visiting the establishment conducted by the firm of Parshley & Co. at No. 72 Main street, for here may be found a large and desirable stock of such goods at prices as low as the lowest. Mr. N. R. Parshley is a native of Middletown and established his present enterprise in 1896. He has built up an extensive business and it is sure to prove permanent, for it is founded on the solid principle of giving full value for every dollar received. The premises make use of comprise one floor of the dimensions of 20 x 85 feet, and is well stocked with a choice selection of men's and boys' fur and wool soft hats in all shapes, also shoes of all kinds, as well as trunks, bags, umbrellas, canes, etc., and a choice line of gents' furnishing goods. Employment is given to two assistants, prompt and courteous attention being assured to every caller.

E. B. Smith, Sanitary Plumber and Heating Engineer; dealer in Crockery, Stoves, Tin-Ware, and House Furnishing Goods; Plumbing, Steam, Water and Mill Supplies; agent for Mills', Gold's, Mahony's and Perfect Steam and Hot Water Boilers; 58 Main Street, Middletown, Conn.— The enterprise carried on by Mr. E. B. Smith was founded in 1870. The premises occupied comprise five floors, each 20 x 85 feet in dimensions, and they are known as the Down Town Crockery Store, as Mr. Smith deals very largely in crockery as well as in stoves, tin-ware, house furnishing goods, and all kinds of drain and sewer pipe, and does a wholesale as well as retail trade. He is also agent for Mills', Gold's, Mahony's and Perfect steam and hot water boilers. Mr. Smith has had a great deal of experience as heating engineer, and with the facilities at his command is in a position to guarantee satisfaction to those who may place orders with him for steam or hot water heating plants of any description. He also makes a specialty of sanitary plumbing in all its details. This gentleman has conducted this business for so long a time in this community, that it is hardly necessary for us to refer to the methods he employs, it being generally understood that they are of the most approved, and thorough in every particular. Those who contemplate steam or hot water heating apparatus, or who wish to give orders for any kind of piping will find it to their advantage to communicate with this house. As the conditions under which such work is to be done, vary in every instance, the importance of securing experienced, conscientious, and expert workmen is plainly seen. Mr. Smith personally superintends all such work and guarantees perfect satisfaction.

Mrs. M. J. H. Chapman, Kandy Kitchen, 120 Main Street, Middletown, Conn.—People have a natural desire to know what they are eating, and therefore a man is entirely excusable for seeking to satisfy himself that whatever enters his mouth is pure and unadulterated. Especially is this true in the case of confectionery, for in the manufacture of this article adulteration has been freely charged, and in some instances proved, and although the wild stories current regarding the introduction of poisonous materials into some candies are entirely imaginary and not founded upon fact, still when a man pays for sugar he wants sugar, and neither "terra alba" nor any other substance however harmless. We are happy to be in a position to call attention to the enterprise conducted by Mrs. M. J. H. Chapman, which was established in 1883. She advertises choice confectionery and ice cream, and as she has been located here for seven years and the trade is steadily growing, no better proof of the purity of the goods she supplies can be desired. If impure ice cream is eaten, the very serious effects which it produces are felt within a few hours, certainly, and as the many who have eaten the ice cream served here have felt no disturbance from so doing, the presumption is, of course, that it is a pure article, made from fresh materials, and proper care is used in the utensils required for its production. The premises required for this business comprise two floors 25x60 feet in dimensions. Eight to ten assistants are employed to serve the numerous patrons in a prompt and satisfactory manner, as the many regular customers can testify.

H. W. Ward (formerly Bailey & Ward), Plumber, Steam and Gas Fitter. Hot Water Heating a Specialty. Tin and Sheet Iron and General Jobbing, 42 Centre Street, Middletown, Conn.—The importance of having such work as steam and gas fitting done by experienced and skillful hands only, would seem to be sufficiently obvious to need no particular mention were it not for the fact that hardly a day passes but what news is circulated of some accident happening owing to steam or gas piping being improperly done. Now there is no necessity for such occurrences, as there are concerns possessed of both the experience and the ability to fill all orders for piping and plumbing in a thoroughly satisfactory and durable manner, and one of the most reliable men engaged in this line of business in Middletown is Mr. H. W. Ward, located at No. 42 Centre street. He was formerly a member of the firm of Bailey & Ward and since 1889 the business has been under the sole management of Mr. H. W. Ward, and now occupies a leading position among similar undertakings in this section. Mr. Ward is a native of Middletown, a member of the Masonic and Odd Fellows fraternities,

and is highly respected throughout the community. A specialty is made of hot water heating and sanitary plumbing, also tin and shee. iron work and general jobbing. Orders for plumbing, steam and gas piping will be given prompt and careful attention at all times, and as four efficient assistants are employed, and the most improved tools and appliances are at hand the most difficult jobs can be undertaken with a guarantee of complete satisfaction and durability.

Thomas B. Bent, Livery and Sale Stables, Coaches, Coupés and Single Teams, No. 26 East Court Street, Middletown, Conn.—Mr. Thomas B. Bent has been sole proprietor of the livery and sale stables at No. 26 East Court street since 1888, but the business was established long before that date, it having been founded many years ago and ranking with the most important enterprises of the kind in this section of the State. The premises utilized are spacious and well arranged, and are equipped with all necessary facilities for carrying on operations to the best advantage. They have a frontage on Court street of 160 feet, and a depth of 90 feet, and the building is three stories in height. The teams furnished by Mr. Bent are decidedly superior to those generally devoted to a livery business, they comparing favorably, in fact, with the average of those from private stables. Coaches, coupés and single teams may be secured here at uniformly reasonable rates and there is no stable in the city at which orders are more promptly and carefully filled, for employment is given to nine assistants and callers are assured immediate and courteous attention. Mr. Bent was born in Middletown and is very generally known throughout this vicinity. The sale department of his business is one of its most noteworthy features, for he is very extensively engaged in the handling of Northern horses and disposes of a great many every year. There are so many and such obvious advantages connected with buying horses of a dealer of Mr. Bent's standing and experience that we will not state them in detail, and indeed the magnitude of his trade shows that the residents of this vicinity fully appreciate his liberal methods, his extensive facilities and his entire responsibility.

F. S. Hills, dealer in Foreign and Domestic Fruits, Groceries and Provisions, Wood and Willow Ware, No. 204 Main Street, Middletown, Conn.—During the long winter months of our trying climate, we are apt to regret that we so ill appreciated the fruits and vegetables that summer ever brings us, and to long for a taste of something fresh and green. This is a feeling to be encouraged rather than crushed, for there is nothing more wholesome than a judicious amount of fruit, and if more people would make the trial, they would discover that instead of being an extravagance, when in winter prices are naturally high, it is an absolute economy, for fruit acts as a tonic, oftentimes averts illness thereby saving much suffering and the inevitable doctor's bills. Fruit is almost a necessity rather than a luxury—it need not be an expensive one, for nobody can see the beautiful oranges sent up from Florida every year, finer by far than those of any other country, and sold at such moderate prices, without acknowledging that they get their money's worth and even more. A choice selection of these and other domestic and foreign fruits is always to be found at the store of Mr. F. S. Hills, 204 Main street. He keeps all kinds of fruit in their season, the best the market affords, besides a large line of groceries, provisions and a variety of articles made of wood and willow ware. Mr. Hills is a native of Franklin, Mass. He started his present business in 1875, and occupies commodious premises, 22 x 105 feet, at 204 Main street, where six attendants are employed who take pleasure in serving all patrons promptly and well. In 1884 Mr. Hills became a member of the common council, serving in that capacity for five years, and now he is one of the city aldermen.

Bailey & Stothart, Plumbers, Steam and Gas Fitters, dealers in Furnaces, Stoves, Ranges, Tinware, Refrigerators, Rubber Hose, Drain Tile, etc. Agents for the "Gurney Hot Water Heater" for Heating Stores, Dwellings and Public Buildings. Tin-roofing and Jobbing of all kinds Promptly Attended to. Estimates Furnished on Application. 97 Main Street, Middletown, Conn.—It is hardly necessary in these days to warn people of the dangers of poor plumbing, for the subjects of drainage and ventilation are continually being improved and are so much before the public, that it seems as if people must pay some attention to them. And yet how often it is we hear of one member of a family after another being stricken with diphtheria, typhus, or some such dire disease, and the cause at last appears to be poor drainage, foul air. Penny wise and pound foolish—for which it is better, to pay the plumber or the doctor? The firm of Messrs. Bailey & Stothart is of recent formation, but the house is an old one of established reputation, dating as far back as 1830, when it was started by Mr. John S. Bailey. The business is retail and of a very comprehensive nature. Plumbing, steam and gas fitting in all their branches, tin-roofing and jobbing of all kinds are done to order, or estimates furnished on application. A large line of furnaces, stoves, ranges and refrigerators are kept constantly in stock, together with rubber hose, drain tile and a variety of tin ware. Messrs. Bailey & Stothart make a specialty of heating stores, dwellings and public buildings, using the "Gurney Hot Water" system, for which they are the agents. The "Gurney" insures a warm house both day and night and is absolutely safe. Nearly twenty of these heaters are in use in this city and vicinity, all of which have given excellent satisfaction. Hot water heating is not an experiment but has been successfully done by the E. & C. Gurney Company in Canada and the United States for twenty years, they being the pioneers in this industry and controlling by patents the most valuable improvements in design of this method of heating. Parties wishing a comfortable and even temperature will do well to consult them. The Model Grand Range for cooking has no equal, and for quick baking, economy and utility we challenge its equal. We can safely say that parties having work to be done in any of the above branches of industry can entrust them to these gentlemen, whose interest it is to do their work satisfactorily. The store is situated at 97 Main street. Three floors of 25×72 feet in dimensions are utilized, besides a small storehouse annexed, and eight competent assistants are employed in the different departments. Both members of the firm are Middletown men and both have from time to time held various local public offices.

C. F. Collins, Banker, dealer in School District Bonds, City Water Bonds, 7 per cent. Debenture Bonds: Office, 134 Main Street, Middletown, Conn.—The handling of investment securities has become a very extensive and important business, for its development has coincided with that of the country, and, indeed, the two are mutually dependent for it is obvious that the natural resources of the country cannot be properly developed without capital, and on the other hand capital cannot be profitably and safely invested in sections where no organized and intelligent system of development is in progress. For obvious reasons, investment securities are best handled by old and well known business men in whom the public have every confidence, and it would be difficult to find a man in this State to whom this description more exactly applies than it does to Mr. C. F. Collins, who has been in active business life for nearly half a century and is universally known and highly esteemed throughout this section. Mr. Collins was in the dry goods business from 1845 to 1855, and then went into the drug business, finally becoming a banker in 1871. He is a high authority on financial matters and has been identified with the management of some of the leading banks of this city, having been one of the organizers of the Central National Bank and a director there for many years; also one of the organizers of the First National Bank and its vice presi-

dent. Mr. Collins has also been secretary of the Sinter & Hall Quarry Co. of Portland for fifteen years, in which company he is quite a large stockholder. Mr. Collins deals in many highly desirable investment securities, such as school district bonds, city water bonds, seven per cent. debenture bonds, etc., and is in a position to render material and valuable assistance to those wishing to place large or small sums of money safely and profitably. He makes a specialty of the negotiation of first mortgage real estate bonds secured on improved farms in the Western States, and paying seven and eight per cent., the principal and interest being guaranteed. These are considered by many competent judges to be the safest investments in this country, and the experience of investors certainly confirms this highly favorable judgment. Some of the most conservatively managed institutions in New England hold these securities, and the most careful and exhaustive investigation will show that the interests of investors are fully protected in every way. Mr. Collins has an office at No. 134 Main street, and will be happy to give detailed information on application, while prompt and painstaking attention will be given to all business placed in his hands.

E. P. Augur, Engineer and Surveyor, 26 Church Street, Middletown, Conn.—One of the best known professional men in Middletown and vicinity is Mr. E. P. Augur, who has an office at No. 26 Church street. This gentleman was born in Middlefield, and has practiced his profession of engineer and surveyor in this city for about a score of years, having been city surveyor of Middletown since 1882. He has a most enviable reputation for giving careful attention to the best interests of his clients, and his work is characterized by that nice consideration of the most minute details and that perfect accuracy which are so essential to the attainment of entirely satisfactory results in such a profession. The general public are hardly in a position to really appreciate the importance of the services rendered by a civil engineer, but it is comparatively easy to set a proper value on the work of a surveyor, for the paramount importance of having the exact boundaries of estates, etc., authoritatively determined is apparent to all. Mr. Augur is in a position to execute commissions at short notice, and city or suburban surveying will be done at very reasonable rates.

C. M. NEWTON,

DEALER IN

Clothing, Hats, Caps, Gent's Furnishing Goods, etc.

214 MAIN STREET. - MIDDLETOWN.

This is a very old stand, but were its age its only recommendation we would not take up the time of our readers in writing about it, for this book has to do with the live concerns of to-day and not with the relics of a bye gone period. But Mr. Newton does not depend upon the past to distinguish his establishment; on the contrary he is fully alive to the demands of the present day and offers inducements to purchasers of clothing, gentlemen's furnishings, etc. The store contains a stock which must truly be seen to be appreciated, for it includes nothing but fresh, seasonable and fashionable goods selected expressly for city trade and sure to give satisfaction to the most critical. The prices, too, are "right" in every respect, and not the least commendable feature of the management is the prompt and polite attention assured to every caller.

The Foster Brothers Co., manufacturers of Padlocks and Small Hardware, Elm St., foot of Court, Middletown, Ct. —Among the various manufacturing enterprises which are the chief cause of Middletown's present prosperity, mention should be made of that conducted by the Foster Brothers Company, manufacturers of some thirty-five styles of padlocks and other small hardware. It was founded in 1878 by the Hedges Hardware Company, and has been carried on under the existing style since 1885. The gentlemen most prominently identified with its management are Messrs. E. R. Foster and C. A. Pelton, the former being a native of New York, and the latter of Middletown, Conn. Mr. Pelton has served on the common council and held various local offices, and both he and Mr. Foster are well known in Middletown and vicinity. The company's productions are favorably known to the trade, as they give the best of satisfaction to consumers and are profitable to handle. The factory is located on Elm street, at the foot of Court street, the premises comprising two floors of the dimensions of 25×75 feet, exclusive of two ells. A well arranged plant of improved machinery is utilized and employment is given to fifteen experienced assistants, the company being in a position to fill all orders promptly and to quote low prices on all the articles manufactured.

Dale D. Butler, General Insurance, office 429 Main Street, Middletown, Conn.—No branch of business in this city or elsewhere has passed through more changes during the last few years than the one now conducted by Dale D. Butler. Although one of the youngest business men in Middletown, Mr. Butler's position is one of the oldest established and most widely known in the State of Connecticut. Maintained successively by J. M. Lanphere, F. E. Camp and A. G. Butler, Mr. Dale D. Butler has succeeded to all the business of his predecessors, and represents as well the People's Fire Insurance Co. Mr. Butler commenced business for himself some four years ago as representative of seven companies. His transactions were eminently successful, and his business during this remarkably short time has grown to such an extent that he now represents twenty-five first-class companies and various life, accident and marine insurance companies. Mr. Butler has unequalled facilities for placing lines in any company that may be preferred by his patrons, and for any amount. As may be imagined, this gentleman is thoroughly well informed on insurance matters of every kind, and it is a matter of fact that he knows more fire, life, marine and accident policies than any other agents in Middlesex county. Mr. Butler's office is centrally located at 429 Main street. Here, any information relating to the intricacies of insurance matters will be cheerfully and courteously given, and we are confident our readers will have reason to thank us for calling their attention and that of the public to this well equipped and popular agency.

HISTORICAL SKETCH OF PORTLAND, CONN.

No settlement was attempted in Portland until some time after the colonists established themselves in Middletown and Cromwell. This was probably on account of the danger of attack from the Indians, and the difficulty of obtaining aid from the colonists across the river. The first settlers who came to Portland were James Stancliff, John Gill and William Cornwall, about the year 1690.

In 1711, a petition signed by thirty-one persons, was sent to the General Court, asking for parish privileges. This was granted, and the parish was named East Middletown, which name it retained until its incorporation with Middle Haddam and East Hampton as a town by the name of Chatham. This latter name was chosen on account of the importance of its ship-building, which industry engrossed the people more and more as time passed on, and in allusion to the town of Chatham in England.

The first vessel built in this place was a schooner of ninety tons, built at Lewis' yard and launched in October, 1741. During the Revolution, many war vessels were built here at the different yards, including the *Trumbull*, *Bourbon*, *Connecticut*, *Holker*, *Macedonian*, *Saranas* and *Boxer*. The *Holker* was built in 1813, and was driven ashore by the English at Narragansett and lost. Another vessel of the same name was built the following year, which was cast away in a storm on the coast of Long Island. No vessels of war have been built in Portland since 1815, nor any ships of equal tonnage.

In 1836, William and Joseph J. Hendly and Alexander Keith of Middletown, and S. Gildersleeve of Portland, built the schooner *William Bryan*, which was the first vessel that ever sailed as a regular packet from New York to Texas. From that vessel has arisen the New York & Galveston Line, which now runs regularly between these ports.

For a long time there were no merchants, stores or manufactures in Portland, the people resorting to Middletown for their necessities, but as quarrying assumed greater importance, other business interests likewise increased. This quarrying had excited more or less attention from the time of the first settlement of Middletown, but ship-building then almost entirely engrossed the minds of the inhabitants, when, after a time, the richness of these quarries was recognized, the name of Chatham was changed to Portland, from Portland, England, from where immense quantities of free stone is

THE CONNECTICUT STEAM BROWN STONE WORKS, PORTLAND.
E. I. Bill, Proprietor. (See page 41).

transported to London and other parts of the country. At first only the stone which had broken off from the cliffs was used. These pieces were sought for building purposes and for grave stones, not only by Middletown people, but by those from other places. Strangers took them as common property and without paying for them, so that in 1665 a law was passed "that no one should dig or raise stones, at the Rocks, on the east side of the river, but an inhabitant of the town, and that twelve pence should be paid to the town, for every ton of stone taken." Soon after this, the stone was

THE SHALER & HALL QUARRY, PORTLAND, CONN.   (See page 39).

considerably sought after and was found valuable for its durability, and for the fine polish it takes. The stone is generally found in layers, from 2 to 18 feet in thickness, varying from 20 to 100 feet in width, and from 50 to 150 feet in length.

Calls are perpetually being made for this stone, from different parts of the country, to be used for large public and private buildings, or for the fronts and ornamental parts of houses and stores. New York, Albany, Philadelphia and Boston have been the principal markets, but this stone has also been carried to Milwaukee, San Francisco and other distant places. It is generally transported by water, the facilities being very great for vessels to draw up at wharves at the foot of the quarries, where they can be laden with comparative ease. Powerful steam engines are

THE CONNECTICUT STEAM BROWN STONE WORKS, PORTLAND.
E. I. BELL, Proprietor. (See page 41)

used for raising the stone, and for pumping out the water which accumulates in the pits. The quarries promise to be a mine of wealth to the inhabitants for many years to come.

The people of Portland joined in the different wars with the other Connecticut troops. Many of them held high military positions ; Col. Blague was a Continental officer, and commanded a company in the battle of Saratoga. It is said that on one occasion General Lafayette presented him with a beautiful sword, in the presence of General Washington.

A curious pond, called Job's Pond, because it is on land formerly owned by Job Payne, is a point of interest and wonder in Portland. It is about two miles in circumference, forty to sixty feet deep, and has no outlet. It rises and falls as much as fifteen feet, but not from the ordinary causes that affect other ponds, for it is often the highest in the dryest season of the year, and lowest in the wet season. When it begins to rise, it rises regularly for six or twelve months, and then falls for about the same period. The reason of this curious phenomenon still remains a mystery.

The situation of Portland is very fine. It is directly opposite Middletown, on the east side of the river, and like that city enjoys an extended and very beautiful view in either direction. There are many fine residences and churches, the streets are broad, picturesque and shaded by enormous trees, and for those who are fond of the country, the drives in the vicinity form a never failing source of enjoyment.

LEADING BUSINESS MEN OF PORTLAND, CONN.

The **Middlesex Quarry Company**, established in 1665, Portland, Conn.—The many advantages which Connecticut brown stone possesses as a building material are so generally known that detailed mention of them is altogether unnecessary, and that some of them at least were appreciated at a very early date in the history of this country, is shown by the fact that the business now carried on by the Middlesex Quarry Company was established away back in 1665. The existing company was organized almost half a century ago, it having been incorporated in 1841, and as the demand for Connecticut brown stone increases with the growth of the country in wealth and culture, it would be a bold man who would set a bound to the development of the great enterprise this company carries on. It has already attained enormous magnitude, the present production averaging about 350,000 feet per annum. As may readily be imagined, the plant in use is very extensive, including among other things thirteen steam boilers and engines, ten buildings, three miles of railroad track, two locomotives, twenty horses and thirty yoke of oxen. The premises owned by the company have an area of between 75 and 100 acres, and have a river frontage of about 4000 feet. Most of the product is shipped by boat but many large orders are shipped by rail, including all those bound for Chicago and points farther west. Employment is given to 512 men, and the quarrying, dressing and shipping facilities are such as to put the company in a position not only to fill the very heaviest orders without delay but to quote the lowest market rates at all times. The material taken from these quarries is remarkable even among Connecticut brown stone for beauty and uniformity of coloring, fineness of grain, ease of working and ability to resist the most severe climate, and what is thought of it by the most eminent architects and builders throughout the country may best be learned from a reading of the following list of some of the more prominent buildings in the construction of which it has been used; Wm. H. Vanderbilt, Frederick Gallatin, Messrs. Twombly & Webb, Wm. H. Fogg, R. S. Stewart, David Dows, Jr., Astor Library, Cooper Union Institute, Union Club and Hotel Normandy, New York City; H. B. Claflin, Brooklyn, N. Y.; Union League Club, Philadelphia, Pa.; Geo H. Corliss, Providence, R. I.; Geo. M. Pullman, H. H. Porter, B. P. Moulton and J. B. Farwell, Chicago, Ill.; Jas. C Flood, San Francisco, Cal., Standard Life Insurance, Montreal, Que ; Western Assurance Co. and Canadian Bank of Commerce, Toronto, Ont.; Canada Life Insurance, Hamilton, Ont.; United States Post Office, Rochester, N. Y., Music Hall, Buffalo, N. Y.; Ætna Fire

Insurance and Soldiers' Memorial, Hartford, Conn. United States Post Office, Middletown, Conn., and United States Post Office and Custom House, Bridgeport, Conn. The company is prepared to contract to furnish brown stone in any desired quantity, the quality to be equal to a fixed standard and the time of delivery to be definitely agreed upon. The various departments of the business are thoroughly systematized and the service is prompt and reliable in the fullest sense of the words. The officers are as follows : President, Henry Gildersleeve ; secretary and treasurer, Charles A. Jarvis ; agent, F. W. Russell ; assistant agent, D. A. Cornwall.

Report by Colt's Patent Fire Arms Manufacturing Co. of tests of the resistance of Portland Stone to gradually applied pressure. The specimens, four in number, in the form of nearly cubical blocks about one and one-half inch square, were received April 12, 1880, from the Middlesex Quarry Company and tested for them. The pressures were applied through steel plates in contact with those surfaces of the block which were parallel to the natural bed of the stone. Except in the case of the specimens of grade No. 1, the stone surfaces were not flat and did not present a full bearing to the pressure plates ; consequently the full strength of the stones of grades 2, 3, and 4, is not given by these tests. The results of the tests are given in the following table in which dimensions are stated in inches, areas in square inches and pressures and resistances in pounds.

TABLE OF RESULTS.

The number of the specimens....	1870	1872	1873	1874
Grade of the stone..............	No. 1	No. 2	No. 3	No. 4
Dimensions of the horizontal cross section of the specimen........	1.57 ×1.57	1.52 ×1.56	1.54 ×1.56	1.54 ×1.56
Area of cross section............	2.53	2.37	2.4	2.4
Height of the specimen.........	1.5	1.47	1.5	1.52
Pressure which produced crushing	97,135	64,454	19,690	15,170
Resistance to crushing per square inch, cross section........	38,393	26,322	8,056	6,322

OFFICE OF COLT'S PATENT FIRE ARMS MFG. CO. }
HARTFORD, April 12, 1880. }
C. B. RICHARDS, Engineer.
W. B. FRANKLIN, Vice President, General Agent.

The Shaler & Hall Quarry Company, Brown Stone, for Stores, Dwellings, Public Buildings, Monuments, etc., furnished to Order, and Shipped to all parts of the United States; also Stone suitable for Rough, Tooled or Hammered Work with Rubble and Junk Stone for Churches, Depots, Forts, Wharves, Bridges, etc., etc. O. W. Mack, Agent. W. H. Edwards, Secretary and Treasurer. Portland, Middlesex County, Conn.—Connecticut brown stone is known in every section of the country, and the best possible evidence of its superiority is that afforded by the steadily increasing demand for it from year to year. A very large amount of capital is invested in quarrying facilities in Portland and vicinity, and one of the most extensive and complete of these plants is that owned by the Shaler & Hall Quarry Company, which was incorporated in 1859, the business with which it is identified having been founded in 1844. Some of the most prominent business men in Connecticut are interested in this representative concern, the president being Mr. J. H. Hall of Hartford, while Mr. W. H. Edwards acts as secretary and treasurer, and Mr. O. W. Mack as agent. The company has built up a most enviable reputation for promptness and accuracy in the filling of orders, and no trouble is spared to fully maintain this reputation in every respect, very extensive and complete facilities being available, and brown stone for stores, dwellings, public buildings, monuments, etc., being furnished to order and shipped to all parts of the United States, together with stone suitable for rough, tooled or hammered work, with rubble and junk stone for churches, depots, forts, wharves, bridges, etc. The area of the premises is about forty acres, and thereon are ten buildings of various sizes, including an office building measuring 25 × 40 feet. Connection is had with the Air Line railroad by a track a mile long owned by the company, which also owns all necessary locomotives, dumping-cars, etc. There are nine steam engines utilized for hoisting purposes, and employment is given to 200 men, who are aided by fifteen horses and twenty-five yoke of oxen. The premises have a river frontage of nearly 2000 feet, and all necessary facilities are provided for loading boats, the larger proportion of the product being shipped in this way. Every order is assured immediate and careful attention, and it is scarcely necessary to add that the company is in a position to quote the lowest market rates on all its products and to faithfully carry out both the letter and the spirit of its agreements.

W. G. Spencer, dealer in Furniture, Paints, Paper Hangings, Oil Cloths, Hardware, Toys, etc., 56 Main St. Portland, Conn.—Mr. Spencer certainly ought to be a good judge of the several commodities which he handles, for he has been the proprietor of this establishment since 1865. His store is very largely patronized, and his customers speak in the highest terms of the uniform reliability of the articles obtained here. Mr. Spencer is a native of Saybrook, and has many friends here, he was a selectman for 1886-8. The premises occupied are located at No. 56 Main street, and comprise two floors each 30 × 75 feet in dimensions. The stock of furniture will be appreciated by those who have had experience in once furnishing their own homes, for its variety and good quality and style. The paints and paper hangings are sold in quantities to suit at low market rates, and the articles handled by Mr. Spencer are obtained from the most reputable manufacturers and will give satisfactory results, if properly used. His stock of oil cloths, hardware, toys, etc., comprise a great variety of everything which can be classed under this head, and they will bear comparison in quality and price with those offered by any other dealer in this line of goods. Mr. Spencer gives employment to three well-informed and competent assistants who are prompt in their attentions to all customers. Goods are cheerfully shown and all orders are carefully and promptly delivered. Mr. Spencer also does quite an extensive undertaking business and in which capacity he has served the people upwards of twenty-five years.

The First National Bank, Portland, Conn.—The First National Bank of Portland has been in operation just about a quarter of a century, it having been incorporated in 1865. During this period the manufactures and commerce of Portland and vicinity have rapidly and steadily developed, and although it would be absurd to say that this development has been brought about by any one cause or by any institution, still there can be no reasonable doubt but that it has been materially aided by the excellent service afforded by the bank in question, and by the confidence which the honorable and enterprising methods employed in its management have inspired. Enjoying favorable relations with other financial institutions throughout the country, the First National is excellently equipped to facilitate exchange, to undertake the collection of drafts, and to discharge the various responsible duties incidental to the carrying on of a general banking business, and the fidelity and despatch with which all commissions are executed have so highly commended the institution to those profiting by the service rendered that it has long ranked with the most popular banks in this section of the State. The discounting of approved commercial paper is one of the most important departments of its business, and as the management is made up of men thoroughly conversant with the standing of local enterprises the bank is in a position to offer needed accommodation without danger to its own interests. The accounts of corporations, institutions, business firms, and individuals are solicited and every depositor may depend upon receiving prompt and reliable service, and having his interests carefully and intelligently protected. The large sum now held on deposit shows that the facilities are appreciated and availed of, and the conservative character of the management is indicated by the existence of a surplus of $30,000, the bank having a capital of $150,000. The banking rooms are conveniently located, and all necessary facilities are at hand to ensure the prompt and accurate transaction of business, employment being afforded to four assistants and callers being given immediate and careful attention. Mr. Henry Gildersleeve is president of the bank, and Mr. Jno. H. Sage, cashier, these gentlemen being associated on the board of directors with other well-known and representative business men.

Ahlquist & Allison, dealers in Groceries, Provisions, Flour, Meal, Feed, Crockery, Glassware, Teas, Coffees, Spices, etc., etc. Agents for Steamship Lines, 46 Main Street, Portland, Conn.—The retail grocery establishments of Portland will compare very favorably as a whole with those of any community in the State, and by no means the least deserving of them is that conducted by Messrs. Ahlquist & Allison, on Main street, for this is a fully stocked and excellently managed grocery store and has fairly won the high degree of popularity it has attained. These gentlemen are both natives of Sweden and they have become well known in this line of business, having founded this enterprise in 1885. They pay especial attention to family trade and their stock is chosen especially for the accommodation of this class of customers, being entirely made up of goods that can be confidently guaranteed to prove as represented. It comprises groceries, provisions, flour, meal, feed, crockery, glassware, teas, coffees, spices, etc., etc., as well as a full line of canned goods, put up by the most reliable packers and warranted pure and wholesome in every respect. There is a regular market price for really dependable groceries, and it would be absurd to assert that this firm is in a position to sell lower than everybody else, but it is the simple truth that they quote rates as low as the lowest, quality considered, and the most experienced buyers, after noting their goods and prices, will agree with us that at no retail grocery in town will a dollar go farther in the purchase of first class goods. The premises occupied comprise two floors each 20 × 50 feet in dimensions. Employment is afforded to five assistants and all orders will receive prompt and accurate attention. These gentlemen are also agents for steamship lines

The Connecticut Steam Brown Stone Works, E. J. Bell, proprietor. Contracts for Brown Stone solicited. Telephone. P. O. Box 500, Portland, Conn.—One of the most prosperous and representative of Portland's various industrial enterprises is the Connecticut Steam Brown Stone Works which have been carried on by Mr. E. J. Bell since 1884. This gentleman is a native of Portland and is very widely known both in business and social circles, he now occupying the position of State representative. The works are very conveniently located as regards the handling of material, the premises utilized having a river frontage of 350 feet and being connected by a spur track with the Air Line railroad. The equipment is first-class in every respect and is very extensive and well arranged, there being two separate and complete manufacturing plants in operation, including two steam-engines of 120 horse power. Three buildings are utilized, their respective dimensions being 100×50, 80×40 and 80×30 feet, and no facility is lacking to enable the most extensive orders to be filled at short notice and in a thoroughly satisfactory manner, employment being given to sixty-three assistants and every department of the business being carried on under skillful and careful supervision. Mr. Bell solicits contracts for brown stone, and is in a position to figure very closely and to deliver goods promptly when promised. Estimates will cheerfully be furnished on application, and as the works have telephone connection communication is easy from any point in this vicinity. Letters should be addressed to P. O. Box 500, and will be given immediate and careful attention.

J. McDonald & Son, Fine Groceries, Provisions, Boots, Shoes, Crockery, Wooden Ware, etc., Portland, Conn.—There are of course many establishments in this town devoted to the sale of groceries, etc., and the task of selecting those truly representative in their character for mention in these columns is not by any means so easy as may at first appear. A representative store is not necessarily a large and pretentious one, and, indeed, some of the most pretentious establishments in Portland are not representative in the slightest degree. But we have no hesitation in calling attention to the enterprise conducted by Mr. J. McDonald & Son, for the policy followed by them is representative of what is best in modern business methods, and highly commends their store to all discriminating purchasers. They offer a very carefully chosen stock of fine groceries, provisions, boots, shoes, crockery, woodenware, etc., and quote prices which prove careful buying and a disposition to be content with a very small margin of profit. Every article sold here is guaranteed to prove precisely as represented, and the assortment is varied enough to allow of all tastes being suited. The premises made use of comprise a store 20 × 60 feet in dimensions, beside room for storage 20 × 90 feet in size.

Miss N. McDonald, Dry and Fancy Goods and Millinery, Main Street, Portland, Conn.—There are quite a number of stores devoted to the sale of dry and fancy goods and millinery, and this one has been known since 1882, for it was then that Miss McDonald started this business here. The premises occupied are 20×30 feet in dimensions, and always contain an attractive assortment of staple articles, as well as a tastefully chosen stock of fashionable novelties in the fancy goods department, which is composed of small wares too numerous to mention here. Miss McDonald devotes her especial attention to the millinery department, and can show a good assortment of hats and bonnets both trimmed and untrimmed, also a large variety of materials from which to select for order work. Miss McDonald is a native of Portland and she has succeeded in obtaining a good share of the custom of this neighborhood. She gives employment to two competent assistants who are courteous and prompt in their service to all. Every effort is made to suit all tastes, and all orders are filled at short notice.

Freestone Savings Bank, Portland, Conn.—"Habit is second nature," according to a familiar saying, and some philosopher has stated that "man is a bundle of habits." Observation confirms the truth of both these sayings, and the wise man is he who, having discovered a truth, utilizes it in his course of conduct. It is comparatively easy to form good habits if one sets about it in the right way, and once formed, all difficulty is at an end for persistence in them becomes mechanical. There for instance is the habit of saving money—one of the most valuable habits any young man can have, for it encourages industry, engenders self-respect and cultivates an honorable and inspiring ambition. As long as a man is making systematic deposits in a savings bank you may be reasonably sure that he has little to be ashamed of in his ways of life, and you may also be sure that he is going to "rise in the world" when opportunity offers. It makes no difference how small his savings may be,—it is the pluck and good sense that enable him to save at all, that single him out from his fellows, and as his earnings increase his savings will increase also. And don't worry about his happiness. Probably he is working hard and not spending much for amusement, but the chances are one hundred to one that he is happier and more contented than though he were earning double the money and spending as fast or faster than he received it. Compare those who deposit their surplus earnings in the Freestone Savings Bank with their fellow workmen who "spend as they go," and see which class is the more intelligent, the more happy and the more respected—and then apply the lesson to your own case. Since the organization of this bank in 1865, it has done a noble work, and to-day is as efficient an aid to good citizenship as can be found in the State. By affording a secure place of deposit for small sums and paying a fair rate of interest on them it does much to encourage saving habits, and the people have excellent reason for the confidence and esteem with which they regard this worthy institution. Its affairs are skillfully and conservatively managed and its financial condition is beyond criticism, the funds being safely and profitably invested and there being a surplus over all liabilities of $14,000. The deposits amount to $329,000 and are steadily increasing, there being many residents of Portland and vicinity who appreciate the advantages of having something laid by for a "rainy day," and know that money entrusted to this representative bank is as safe as it possibly can be. The president is Mr. F. Gildersleeve, and the treasurer is Mr. Jno. H. Sage, they being assisted in the management of affairs by other well-known business men.

C. E. Blodgett, dealer in Drugs, Medicines, Chemicals and Fancy Goods, Portland, Conn.—Among the many attractive business enterprises of Portland none are more deserving of notice than the above named store, which is an old establishment, situated in a good location, having been founded by the present proprietor in 1876, and which has gained an enviable position in the trade. The premises occupied are 20 × 50 feet in dimensions, they are nicely fitted up and convenient, the stock embraces a full and complete line of drugs, chemicals, medicines and fancy goods, together with an assortment of such specialties as are usually to be found in a first class pharmacy. The display of case goods and the many fancy articles rival those shown by many of his competitors, and the prescription department is conducted with a skill and intelligence which has given the house an enviable reputation in this vicinity. Among the many useful and highly recommended preparations, which he carries, special mention is made of Blodgett's Celebrated Witch Hazel Cream. A full line of cigars, tobacco, and confectionery may also be found here. Mr. C. E. Blodgett, who was born in Stafford, Conn., is well and favorably known and is a director in the First National Bank. The services of two efficient and thoroughly competent clerks are secured, and every effort is made to give accurate attention to every customer.

The Brainerd Quarry Co., Connecticut Brown Stone. Building and Monument Stone of any size, and in any quantity, furnished to order. Good Coarse Stone, suitable for Churches, Bridges, Docks, Piers, etc. Also Rubble or Wall Stone. Vessels always in readiness at the quarry, Portland, Conn.—Stone has been taken from the quarries now controlled by the Brainerd Quarry Company for 225 years, so that the extensive business now carried on by the concern in question may be said to have been founded in 1665. Many other deposits of brown stone have been discovered since that date, but the comparative position now held by that quarried by this company is indicated by the award decreed by the United States Centennial Commission, December 4, 1876, "for the good color, uniform texture, and durability of the Connecticut Brown Stone from the Portland quarries." The Brainerd Quarry Company was incorporated in 1879, the president being Mr. E. Brainerd, and the secretary and treasurer, Mr. LeRoy Brainerd. Both these gentlemen are natives of Portland, and are so generally known in business and social circles as to make extended personal mention entirely unnecessary. The company utilize premises having an area of about fifty acres and a river frontage of 2000 feet. Fifteen vessels of from 150 to 400 tons burden are required to transport the product during the working season, the shipping facilities being so extensive as to admit of the loading of from three to four vessels per day. The quarrying facilities are on an equally large scale, six engines being used for drilling, etc., and employment being given to 300 men, aided by thirty-four horses and forty yoke of oxen. The company are prepared to furnish Connecticut Brown Stone for all purposes in quantities to suit, including building and monument stone of any size, and good coarse stone, suitable for churches, bridges, docks, piers, etc. Rubble or wall stone will also be supplied at the lowest market rates, and as the productive facilities are ample, and vessels are always in readiness at the quarry the largest orders can be filled at short notice.

Strong & Hale, dealers in Lumber and Builders' Materials, a Complete Stock of Builders' Hardware, Oils, Varnishes, Turpentine and Colors, Lime, Cement and Hair, Doors, Sash, Blinds, etc., South End Main Street, Adjoining Ferry, Portland, Conn.—The establishment conducted by Messrs. Strong & Hale is the only one of the kind in town, but should such of our readers as are not familiar with Portland and vicinity conclude from this that the residents of that section did not enjoy equal advantages in the purchase of building materials with other communities they would make a great mistake, for the firm in question carry an extremely heavy and varied stock, fill orders accurately and promptly and quote bottom prices on all the many commodities in which they deal. This business has been carried on for more than a score of years, it having been founded in 1869 by Messrs. Taylor & Hale, who were succeeded in 1871 by Messrs. Taylor & Strong, the present firm assuming control in 1879. The partners are Messrs. E. B. Strong and A. H. Hale, both of whom are natives of Portland. The premises made use of have an area of one and a half acres and are located at the south end of Main street, next to the ferry. There are several buildings utilized for sale and storage purposes, the largest containing two floors of the dimensions of 30x90 feet. As before remarked, the stock on hand is exceptionally large and varied, and as Messrs. Strong & Hale do both a wholesale and retail business, they are prepared to fill the heaviest orders without delay and to give the smallest orders prompt and careful attention. Among the most important commodities dealt in may be mentioned lumber and builders' materials, including a complete line of builders' hardware, oils, varnishes, turpentine and colors, lime, cement and hair, doors, sash, blinds, etc. Special inducements are offered to parties ordering by the car load, and in every department of the business the firm are well prepared to successfully meet all honorable competition, both as regards quality of the goods and lowness of the prices quoted.

Geo. W. Lord, The Portland Pharmacy, Portland, Conn.—"The Portland Pharmacy" has gained a substantial position among the first class prescription drug stores located in this neighborhood. Mr. Geo. W. Lord who is a native of Coventry, Conn., began operations here in 1886, and his record from the first has been such as to inspire confidence in the method of the management. A very complete stock of drugs, medicines and chemicals is carried, and the most approved facilities are at hand for the compounding of physicians' prescriptions, to which particular attention is given. Absolute accuracy is ensured by the carefully considered system employed, and orders are filled at short notice, as well as at uniformly moderate rates. The premises are 20 x 35 feet in dimensions and contain a good assortment of such goods as are generally found in a first-class family drug store. One competent and careful assistant is employed and prompt and courteous attention is extended to all. Mr. Lord puts up for wholesale and retail trade the famed "Cherry Rock Cough Syrup," which is unsurpassed for coughs, colds, hoarseness, sore throat, bronchitis, and all diseases of the throat and lungs. Mr. Lord is doing an extensive business with this well tried and valuable article.

John Sarsfield, dealer in House Furnishing Goods, Paints and Oil; Wall Paper, Oil Cloth, etc. Undertaking in all its branches. First store south of Edward's Block, Portland, Conn.—Although it is unquestionably true that some men may carry on a certain line of business for many years, and still be less expert in it than others who have had but comparatively limited experience, this does not alter the fact that he who has been longest engaged in a certain field of action, is apt to be in a position to offer peculiar and decided inducements to patrons. Many instances might be brought forward in proof of this, but we will simply refer to the advantages held out by Mr. John Sarsfield, carrying on operations on Main street. This gentleman is a native of this town, and having started this business here in 1878, he has become prominent in business, as well as in social circles. The premises utilized comprise two floors each 20 x 50 feet in dimensions, which are well filled with house furnishing goods, which includes furniture of all styles and all makes, and which will suit all tastes and purses. He has a large assortment of wall paper and oil cloth of new and desirable designs, also paints and oil of a superior quality. He has also on hand a good variety of coffins, caskets, etc., and he is prepared to attend to any orders for undertaking in all its branches, having every modern facility at hand for conducting this business in a satisfactory and thorough manner. All orders are assured immediate and careful attention. Residence over Chas. Beardon's store. Night calls promptly attended to by calling at residence.

William Walsh, dealer in Choice Groceries, Provisions, Flour, Meal and Feed. A full line of Teas, Coffees and Spices. Marlborough Street, Portland, Conn.—There is a proverb to the effect that the only way to make sure that a thing is properly done is to do it yourself, and although of course such advice is not always practical still there is no doubt that it is founded on sound principles. Those who do business with Mr. William Walsh, on Marlborough street, frequently remark upon the promptness, courtesy, intelligence and reliability of the service at that popular store, and the reason why callers are so satisfactorily attended to is simply because the proprietor gives personal attention to every detail of his business, and hence being sure that it will be well done. Mr. Walsh has carried on his present enterprise since 1885. Premises measuring 40 x 50 feet are utilized, and a heavy and varied stock is carried, made up of choice groceries, provisions, flour, meal and feed. He also carries a full line of teas, coffees and spices. He quotes the lowest market rates on all these commodities, and makes it a point to furnish goods that will give entire satisfaction. He is rapidly increasing his business and fully deserves the success he has thus far attained. Employment is afforded to two assistants.

John Bransfield, dealer in Fine Groceries, Provisions and General Merchandise, Coal and Wood, Blue Stone Flagging and Curbing. Corner Main Street and Air Line Avenue, Portland.—The business carried on by Mr. John Bransfield at the corner of Main street and Air Line avenue, was founded in 1872 by Messrs. Bransfield & Condon, but since 1874 has been under the exclusive control of the present proprietor, who is a native of Portland, has held various local offices, and is too well known throughout this vicinity to make extended personal mention necessary. The premises utilized have an area of three acres, and the main store building has a frontage of 100 feet and a depth of 60 feet, thus affording ample room for the accommodation of a very heavy and varied stock, comprising choice staple and fancy groceries, provisions, and a full line of general merchandise. Mr. Bransfield also deals largely in coal and wood, and blue stone flagging and curbing, employing twelve assistants in the various departments of his business, and being prepared to fill all orders at short notice and to quote prices as low as the lowest. He gives the enterprise careful personal supervision and insists upon uniform courtesy being shown to every customer, the result being that the establishment is popular among both large and small buyers and receives an extensive and constantly increasing patronage. Of course it would be quite impossible to give a detailed description of the stock carried within the limited space at our command, so we will simply say that it is exceptionally complete in every department, so that all tastes and all purses can be suited. It is Mr. Bransfield's policy to sell goods strictly on their merits, and every article bought of him is guaranteed to prove just as represented in every respect. In addition to the foregoing articles dealt in, Mr. Bransfield sells all kinds of farming utensils, among which is the famous Buckeye mowing machine, Yankee horse rake, Bullard hay tedder, fertilizers of all kinds, a specialty being made of Williams, Clark & Co.'s high grade bone fertilizers, ground land plaster and soluble guano.

Mrs. M. A. McDonald, dealer in Dry and Fancy Goods, Main Street, Portland, Conn.—We have no intention of denying that there are many advantages gained by patronizing the enormous dry goods stores which have come into existence of late years, for the fact that they are supported by the purchasing public shows that some inducements are offered at least, but the same public have lately begun to appreciate the fact that a small and well managed store may be made more desirable to patronize than these vast establishments to which we have referred. Take for instance the store conducted by Mrs. M. A. McDonald on Main street, and you find a carefully selected and varied stock, comprising the latest fashionable novelties, complete in every department, and made up of goods which are offered at very reasonable rates. Instead of wandering about in an immense building, you can sit down in a cosy store and make your selections with some comfort, and the prompt and courteous attention given you is of itself something worth considering. These points are worth considering, and they have caused many people to return to their original practice of buying of comparatively small dealers. Mrs. McDonald is a native of this town and founded her present business in 1877. The premises utilized are 20x50 feet in size. She gives her close personal attention to this business, and is constantly striving to improve the service rendered, and fully deserves the success already attained.

Richard O'Brien, dealer in Groceries, Provisions and Ship Stores, Main Street, near Ferry, Portland, Conn.—Considered from some standpoints eleven years is a very long time, while from others it seems but a brief period after all. But however long or short a time it may seem, the fact remains that few business houses attain so high a position in the estimation of the public in eleven years as

has that conducted by Mr. Richard O'Brien. This gentleman is a native of New Haven, and founded this enterprise in 1879. He has resorted to no illegitimate or questionable methods to build up his business, but has proceeded from the first on the good old fashioned principle of giving a dollar's worth for a dollar, and assuring equal and equitable treatment to all. The premises utilized are 25 x 60 feet in dimensions, and the stock on hand is made up of groceries, provisions and ship stores, selected especially for this trade, and it contains a large assortment of all goods usually found in such establishments. The prices quoted on many articles handled are as low as can be named by any dealer in this line of trade. All orders are strictly and promptly attended to at short notice.

James Laverty, wholesale dealer in Wines, Liquors, Ales, Cigars, etc., Portland, Conn.—The establishment conducted by Mr. James Laverty on Main street is one of the best equipped and best known in this section of the State. The proprietor is an old resident of Portland, and to his case extended personal mention is quite unnecessary, for he has a very large circle of friends throughout this vicinity and has long been regarded as one of our most enterprising and truly representative business men. The premises utilized by him have an area of 3900 square feet, and contain an exceptionally large and complete stock of wines, liquors, ales, etc., together with a full assortment of foreign and domestic cigars, including many of the most popular brands. An extensive wholesale and retail business is done, and as employment is given to five competent assistants, callers are assured prompt and courteous attention. Mr. Laverty enjoys the most favorable relations with producers and is consequently in a position to quote low prices on all the articles he handles, and to supply goods that will give satisfaction to the most fastidious. His stock is so varied that all tastes can easily be suited, and particular attention is paid to handling wines, liquors and cordials especially adapted to medicinal and family use. There is an active demand for pure liquors of all kinds and the present magnitude of Mr. Laverty's business is due in a great measure to the care he takes to furnish goods that are positively free from all adulteration. A first-class livery is connected with the establishment, and good teams may be had at short notice and at very reasonable rates. The horses, carriages, etc., are kept in excellent condition and those who enjoy driving but have no teams of their own, cannot do better than to make frequent use of the facilities here provided.

Patrick Sullivan, dealer in Choice Family Groceries, Provisions, Wood, Hay and Straw, Boots, Shoes and Rubbers, Main Street, near Air Line Avenue, Portland, Conn.—The difference between a family grocery and an ordinary grocery, has never been satisfactorily explained and probably never will be, for there are some things which can be appreciated and yet cannot be successfully put into words, and this is one of them. The true family grocery is carried on with particular regard to the requirements of family trade, the stock being carefully chosen and no pains being spared to furnish goods that will give entire satisfaction. We question if a more perfect type of this kind of a grocery can be found in this section than that of which Mr. Patrick Sullivan is the proprietor, located on Main street, and judging from the extent and character of the support given this house there are many others holding a similar opinion. Mr. Sullivan founded his present enterprise in 1872, and he is extremely well known personally in Portland and vicinity. The premises made use of are 40 x 25 feet in dimensions besides a storehouse 30x24 and another 16x15 feet, and contain a large and varied stock, comprising choice family groceries, provisions, wood, hay and straw, boots, shoes and rubbers, all these articles being offered at the lowest market rates. Mr. Sullivan employs four assistants and every order is assisted immediate and painstaking attention.

P. Mulcahy, dealer in Groceries, Provisions, Flour, Meal, Feed, Wooden and Glass Ware and Crockery, Canned Goods, Teas, Coffees and Spices. Opposite Air Line Depot, Portland, Conn.—There are very few things in the line of family food supplies which cannot be obtained at the establishment conducted by Mr. P. Mulcahy, for he deals in groceries, provisions, flour, meal, feed, teas, coffees and spices. He also carries a full line of canned goods, and a large assortment of wooden and glass ware and crockery. He keeps his assortment complete in every department and while sparing no pains to handle goods that will suit all, he quotes prices that will satisfy the most economically disposed. Mr. Mulcahy

founded the business he now carries on in 1888, and he has already built up a patronage which is bound to continue to increase as long as the residents of Portland appreciate liberal and honorable business methods. This house caters to all classes of trade and gives as much attention to small as to large customers, the result being that this store is one of the most popular of its kind in this section. Orders are promptly and accurately filled, and the buyer has the satisfaction of knowing that he will get full value for every penny that he pays out. The premises, which are located opposite the Air Line Depot, comprise two floors each 40x60 feet in dimensions. Employment is given to two capable assistants.

HISTORICAL SKETCH OF MIDDLEFIELD, CONN.

(ROCKFALL AND BAILEYVILLE)

The first settlers located in Middlefield about the year 1700, and when the society was incorporated in October, 1744, there were more than fifty families within its limits, the aggregate list of whose property exceeded £3,000, so that Middlefield early proved an attractive place. Almost all these people were farmers, and from this time the population did not vary greatly for many years. Toward the close of the eighteenth century, however, the important water privileges on West River and especially on the tributary to this stream, induced numbers to engage here in manufacturing, and from that time on the population has been steadily increasing. The people built their first meeting-house in 1745, forty feet square. The ancient records of this church are lost, but it was probably organized by the same council that ordained the first pastor, Rev. Ebenezer Gould, October 10, 1747. The third minister settled here was Rev. Abner Benedict, a graduate of Yale. He was an able divine and a man of strong affections and while in Middlefield, about the close of the Revolutionary War, accomplished, by his address and efforts the freedom of all the slaves held by the people.

The Methodist Church commenced work here in 1791, and in 1844 built their first church.

There are two post-offices within the limits of Middlefield—one at Middlefield Center and one at Rockfall, which latter village was set off as a separate district of Middlefield in 1832. Here, at Rockfall, was erected a powder mill as early as 1793, and in 1798 a factory for cutting nails, which is believed to have been the first instance of nail cutting by machinery in this country.

The fall is one of the largest and finest waterfalls in Connecticut, and just above it is located a large mill of the Russell Manufacturing Co. The river makes a bend here and the volume of light green water rushes first over a V-shaped dam, then almost immediately breaks into white foam masses on the rocks of the fall, while through the spray and mist below you may see the prismatic colors of the rainbow.

Middlefield was incorporated in 1866, when by act of legislature it was set off from Middletown. No alcohol is sold here and since the organization of the town, the municipal and war debts have been paid and also a large part of the railroad indebtedness, so that the town is in good financial condition. The Air Line railroad runs through it and the place has always been regarded as very healthy, the proportion of deaths to population being unusually small.

LEADING BUSINESS MEN OF MIDDLEFIELD.

(BAILEYVILLE AND ROCKFALL).

Chas. P. Burnham, dealer in Groceries and Provisions, Baileyville, Town of Middlefield, Conn.—Although it is doubtless true that "smart" methods of doing business may be successful for a time, even if they are employed at the expense of reliability, still it is undeniable that permanent success is to be gained but in one way—the "old-fashioned" methods of giving full value for money received. The fact is well worthy of consideration by young men who contemplate going into business for themselves, and if they want a prominent example practically demonstrating its truth, they can find one in the establishment conducted by Mr. C. P. Burnham for it would not be possible to name an enterprise occupying a higher position in the esteem of the residents of Middlefield and vicinity. A heavy stock of general merchandise is constantly on hand, comprising choice groceries, provisions, etc., also coal, and employment is given to four efficient assistants, thus assuring prompt attention to every customer. Mr. Burnham's long experience and very favorable relations with producers, etc., enables him to quote the lowest market rates in every department of his business, and the surety customers have of getting just what they pay for has much to do with the character and extent of the trade enjoyed. Mr. Burnham has been identified with his present enterprise since 1884. He is a Connecticut man by birth and is universally known throughout this section on account of his pronounced business ability.

Otis A. Smith, manufacturer of Revolvers, Bench Planes, Carpenters' Tools and Hardware Specialties, Rockfall, Conn. One of the most thoroughly equipped of the many manufacturing establishments to be found in this section of the State is that conducted by Mr. Otis A. Smith at Rockfall. This business was founded some thirty years ago, and its present magnitude is the legitimate result of the enterprising and honorable methods which have characterized its management from the first, for consumers and the trade have long since learned that entire dependence can be placed upon Mr. Smith's productions and as a natural consequence the demand for them is constant and steady. The premises occupied comprise three floors of the dimensions of 60 x 70 feet, and are fitted up with improved machinery, driven by water-power. Among the most prominent productions may be mentioned revolvers, bench planes and carpenters' tools, together with a variety of **hardware** specialties embracing **some** very useful novelties. **The** market is so flooded nowadays with cheaply and poorly made revolvers that the only way to be sure of getting a reliable and durable weapon is to insist upon being supplied with one made by some reputable manufacturer, and Mr. Smith has the reputation of producing revolvers that are unsurpassed for accuracy, simplicity and durability. His bench planes and carpenters' tools are also thoroughly made from selected material and will give the best of satisfaction in every instance. Employment is given to forty experienced assistants, and the most extensive orders can be filled at short notice and at prices as low as the lowest, quality considered.

C. P. Bonfoey, dealer in Groceries and Provisions, Rockfall, Conn.—It is true that often what is of great interest to one man may have no attraction for another, but there are some subjects in which all are interested to a greater or less degree, and among these may be placed those relating to where reliable goods may be bought to the best advantage. Therefore we feel sure that our readers will not begrudge the time spent to learning a little concerning the establishment conducted by Mr. C. P. Bonfoey located at Rockfall, near Middletown, Conn., for this is certainly a store where a large stock is carried, a various assortment offered, and low prices quoted. Here is a combination of advantages worthy of careful consideration, and we **are** convinced that the more thoroughly the inducements here offered are investigated, the more solid and substantial they will be proved. Mr. Bonfoey handles a large assortment of goods, dealing in choice groceries and provisions. His stock is made up of both staple and fancy articles, and is selected expressly for family use, being obtained from the most reliable sources. The fact that the prices will bear comparison with those of any other dealer in this section has a great deal to do with the large retail business done. Two competent assistants are constantly employed and ensure prompt and civil attention to every customer, and it should be especially noted that Mr. Bonfoey guarantees every article sold at his establishment to prove precisely as represented. He is a native of Connecticut and is well and favorably known throughout Rockfall and vicinity.

STREET IN DURHAM CENTRE, CONN.

HISTORICAL SKETCH OF DURHAM CENTRE, CONN.

When the towns of Middletown, Haddam, Killingworth and Guilford were first surveyed, a tract of unclaimed land was discovered, lying between them. After a time this was divided into farms, which the colonial legislature presented to distinguished men for special services rendered. This territory was known as Coginchaug, so named by the original owners, the Mattabesett Indians, who used it as a hunting-ground. It is traversed by several streams, the principal one being the Coginchaug or Arawansit, which joins the Little River in Middletown.

In May, 1699, a petition was sent to the General Court, sitting in Hartford, requesting that Coginchaug might be made a township. This petition was granted, and in 1704 the Indian name was changed to Durham, and two years later the first town meeting was held.

The first ecclesiastical society was formed in 1708, with the Rev. Nathaniel Chauncey as pastor.

Durham sympathized strongly with the Mother Country during the French War, and sent a considerable number of volunteers. Colonel Elihu Chauncey of this place, commanded a regiment in the year 1755, and Major-General Phineas Lyman, another prominent Durham man, was commander-in-chief of the Connecticut troops during a portion of the war.

Durham also entered into the Revolutionary War with zeal and patriotism. Almost every able-bodied man in the town, from the ages of sixteen to sixty, was in the service at one time or another, many of them being highly distinguished for their bravery. Among these was James Wadsworth, Jr., who was appointed brigadier-general during this war.

It is said that during the Civil War, from 1861 to 1864, Durham was represented in seventeen regiments, and paid nearly $13,000 toward the support of the troops.

Naturally, the first occupation of the people was agriculture and farming, followed later by the exchange of articles of agricultural produce, for which they received merchandise, sugar, molasses, rum and sometimes negroes, for slaves were owned in Durham, as in other Connecticut towns.

Manufacturing has developed more slowly in Durham than in most of the neighboring towns. They are still mainly a farming people, with some manufacturing interests.

LEADING BUSINESS MEN OF DURHAM CENTRE, CT.

Henry Davis, Dry Goods, Groceries, Boots and Shoes, Hardware, Tinware, Agricultural Implements and Feed, Durham Centre, Conn.—The store (see previous page), conducted by Mr. Henry Davis is very popular among the residents of this vicinity, and one does not have to seek far to find the reasons for this state of affairs, it is evident from very little observation that the stock carried is an exceptionally complete and desirable one, and the prices quoted on the goods composing it, are of themselves enough to ensure its frequent renewal, while the prompt and polite attention given to every customer completes the favorable impression made by the goods and the prices. The establishment in question was inaugurated in 1873 by H. Davis & Co., and so conducted until 1875, when Mr. Henry Davis assumed entire management. He is a native of Killingworth, Conn., and is very well known and highly respected in Durham and vicinity. He was State Representative in 1878, and has also been selectman and held other local offices. No detailed description of the stock carried by Mr. Davis is possible within our limited space, but speaking generally, it may be said to be made up of dry goods, groceries, boots and shoes, hardware, tin ware, agricultural implements and feed. The premises utilized are centrally located and comprise two floors each 24 × 36 feet in dimensions, in addition to a feed room 16 × 36 feet in size. Three courteous and well informed assistants are employed, and all goods sold here are guaranteed to prove just as represented, and no trouble is spared to completely satisfy every customer.

W. A. Parsons & Co., manufacturers of Stationer's Tin Hardware, Cash Boxes, Safe Deposit Boxes, etc. Special Size and Shape Boxes made to order at short notice. Estimates furnished upon application. Durham Centre, Conn.—Many efforts have been made to introduce substitutes for the tin cash boxes, document boxes, letter and bill head boxes, etc., so popular with the business public, but no appreciable degree of success has been attained, for the simple reason that none of these substitutes possessed the good qualities of the articles they were intended to supersede. The cost of tin boxes has been considerably reduced of late by improved methods of manufacture and as a consequence they are now in more active demand than ever before. Messrs W. A. Parsons & Co. make a specialty of the production of stationers' tin hardware, cash boxes, safe deposit boxes, etc., and their goods are conceded to be unsurpassed for strength, convenience and neatness. The firm utilize spacious and well equipped premises and employ experienced workmen, being in a position to fill orders at short notice and at the lowest market rates. Operations were begun in 1884, the partners being Messrs. W. A. Parsons and George J. Francis, both of whom are widely known in this vicinity, especially the former, who at present holds the position of State representative. The firm are prepared to make special sizes and shapes to order at short notice, and will promptly furnish estimates on application. They do both a retail and jobbing business and large and small orders are assured equally careful attention.

W. J. Atwell, Livery and Feed Stable, Durham Center, Conn.—There's many a cure for disease not to be found in any apothecary store, and it may be added that the same may be said of preventatives of it. Fresh air, rapid motion, and the exhilaration attending driving are oftentimes more potent than any drugs in straightening a man out, and if more frequent use were made of them by our overworked business men, some of our physicians could safely take a holiday. We believe that people are beginning to appreciate this fact, and to guide such as may feel uncertain as to where they can secure a desirable team at a fair rate, we would suggest a visit to the establishment of Mr. W. J. Atwell, located in Durham Center. Mr. Atwell is possessed of the means to assure his patrons the best service in every respect. He takes a pride in furnishing such horses and carriages as no one need be ashamed of, and although he does not pretend to have a Maud S. in his stable, still he does strive to furnish good roadsters as well as stylish appearing animals. The premises in use comprise two floors each 25 × 30 feet, and an office building 10 × 16 feet in dimensions, and offer the best of accommodations to horses and the most intelligent care is promised. Reasonable rates are adhered to, and satisfaction is assured. Mr. Atwell is a native of this town and has been identified with his present enterprise since 1883. Mr. Atwell is also proprietor of the stage route between Durham and Middlefield station, carrying the mail and passengers, also express stuff, making two regular trips daily. He also makes three regular trips weekly, Tuesday, Thursday and Saturday, to Middletown, doing errands and carrying passengers.

Merriam Mfg. Co., manufacturers of Stationers' Tin Goods, Tin Toys, Japanned and Stamped Tin Ware, House Furnishing Goods, Toilet Ware, etc., Durham, Conn.—The business carried on by the Merriam Manufacturing Company was founded nearly forty years ago, the company having been organized in 1851, by Messrs. L. T. Merriam & Co. of Meriden, and some prominent business men of Durham. Mr. S. S. Scranton is president of the company, and Mr. Frank Hubbard is secretary and treasurer. A number of important specialties are manufactured, such as stationers' tin goods, tin toys, japanned tin ware, house furnishing goods, toilet ware, etc., and these productions are very generally and favorably known to consumers and the trade, they being carefully and strongly made and differing widely from much of the tin ware now so common in the market. The premises utilized comprise three buildings connected, one being two stories in height and 120 × 24 feet in dimensions, another two stories high and 24 × 70 feet in size, and another one story high and measuring 24 × 30 feet. Improved machinery is used, including a fifty-horse boiler and a fifteen-horse engine. Employment is given to from twenty to twenty-five assistants, and the most extensive orders can be filled at very short notice and at low rates. One of the most popular specialties is the Merriam Manufacturing Company's snak handle cash box. This is made in sizes varying from seven to eighteen inches, the boxes being furnished with assorted tumbler locks and being substantially and neatly made in every detail. They are very popular among business men and are desirable for any stationer to handle, as they sell at a moderate figure and give the best of satisfaction.

S. W. Fowler, dealer in Choice Family Groceries, Teas, Coffees, Spices, Drugs and Medicines. Extract of Witch-Hazel by the pint, quart or gallon. Durham Centre, Conn. —The vastness and importance of the grocery trade of Connecticut can scarcely be over estimated, and the total quantity of these goods retailed in the course of the year must be something enormous. Each section of the State has certain houses which are conceded to be leaders in their several lines, and so far as Durham Centre is concerned, the establishment conducted by Mr. S. W. Fowler, must be given a high position. This enterprise was founded in 1881 by Fowler Brothers, and since 1888 has been under the sole management of its present proprietor, Mr. S. W. Fowler. This undertaking has been steadily extended since its inception, for the methods practiced have been at once enterprising and conservative, and such as could not fail to inspire confidence and attract patronage. An extensive retail business is done, two assistants being required to serve the many patrons, and the filling of orders, etc. The premises utilized are 26 × 30 feet in size and are stocked with a large and varied assortment of goods, including choice family groceries, teas, coffees and spices; also drugs and medicines. The prices are very reasonable and economy is best served in the long run by trading at a representative establishment like this. Mr. Fowler, who is a native of Guilford, Conn., is very widely known and highly respected in Durham Centre. He was State Representative in 1878, and has held various other offices in town. He respectfully solicits patronage, and assures prompt attention to, and accurate delivery of orders as promised.

M. F. Stanhope, General Family Supply Bazaar, Durham, Conn.—If the word "bazaar" be defined to mean an establishment where goods in great variety are sold at lowest prices we believe that no one familiar with the facts would question the justice of its application to the emporium conducted by Mr. M. F. Stanhope in Durham, under the style of general family supply bazaar. This gentleman may be entitled one of the leaders in this line of trade in Durham, and it would be difficult to find a man more thoroughly posted, or one more alive to the demands of the times. He began business in 1885, and during the time since elapsed he has built up a reputation for low prices and fair dealings. He is a native of Providence, R. I., and is one of our most widely known local merchants. Two floors are occupied, each 20 × 35 feet in dimensions, and a stock is carried which is hard to parallel elsewhere, either for size or variety, and includes a hundred and one articles which our limited space will not admit of mention. Well-informed, reliable and courteous assistants are employed, and the entire business is conducted by Mr. Stanhope on a high plane of honor and fair representation of all goods and one price, that the lowest.

Wellman & Newton, dealers in Dry Goods, Groceries, Hardware, Crockery, Boots and Shoes, Paper Hangings and Notions, Flour, Feed and High Grade Fertilizers, Durham, Conn.—There is no use in trying to describe such a stock as is carried by Messrs. Wellman & Newton in detail. We to begin with our space is not half large enough and then again it is not to be fully described in words anyway. The only thing to do is to go see it yourself. The tim there so far will not be wasted by any means, for the goods are so varied in kind that you will surely find something you need among them and the prices are so low that there is no fear but what you will get the full worth of your money, whether you spend ten cents or ten dollars. This is one of the best known and oldest established enterprises in Durham, it having been inaugurated in 1853 by Mr. J. W. Leach. The present firm is composed of Mr. F. L. Wellman, and Mr. F. S. Newton, both natives of Durham. The premises made use of are very spacious, comprising a store 30 × 60 feet in dimensions, and two storehouses. These being none too large to accommodate the immense and varied stock dealt in, which includes dry goods, groceries, hardware, crockery, boots and shoes, paper hangings, notions, etc.; also flour, feed, and high grade fertilizers, and the stock is always kept complete in every department. Three competent assistants are employed and every caller is assured immediate and courteous attention.

G. T. Nettleton, dealer in Beef, Mutton, Pork, Poultry, etc., Durham Centre, Conn.—The importance of the meat and provision trade cannot be over estimated, for it is truly one of the most prominent industries, engaging the attention of a large number of firms and individuals, and employing labor and capital to a marked degree. Through thousands of tons of these commodities are sold each year, there is no perceptible diminution in the demand for first-class goods. Among the several houses devoted to the above-named line of business in Durham Center, that of Mr. G. T. Nettleton occupies an honorable position. Mr. Nettleton is a native of Durham Center and established his business in 1889. The premises utilized measure 18 × 28 feet, and are filled with a large and well selected stock of choice meats, poultry, etc., and a large variety of fruits and vegetables in their season. The large trade of this house requires the services of two thoroughly competent assistants, and its details are most ably managed in conducting a business of this kind great judgment is required in keeping a proper quantity, as well as quality of goods on hand, as the seasons change so suddenly and the demands of the public vary with each change. All the goods of this house are always renovated, and all purchasers are too well aware of their extra quality to oblige us to call special attention to them. By continued efforts to please all customers, the popularity of this house must necessarily increase rapidly. Mr. Nettleton keeps a full supply of Western and home butchered beef constantly on hand. He also does custom butchering.

INDEX TO BUSINESS NOTICES.

www.ingramcontent.com/pod-product-compliance
Lightning Source LLC
Chambersburg PA
CBHW031808090426
42739CB00008B/1218